GHOSTS OF
COLORADO SPRINGS
AND PIKES PEAK

GHOSTS OF COLORADO SPRINGS AND PIKES PEAK

STEPHANIE WATERS

HAUNTED
AMERICA

Published by Haunted America
A Division of The History Press
Charleston, SC 29403
www.historypress.net

Copyright © 2012 by Stephanie Waters
All rights reserved

Front cover: The Pioneer Museum. *Photo courtesy of Sita Ahlen.*

First published 2012

Manufactured in the United States

ISBN 978.1.60949.467.4

Library of Congress CIP data applied for.

Dedicated to my storytelling muses and mentors:
Grandma Jessie, and my dear friend Hope "Bunny" Hall.

CONTENTS

ACKNOWLEDGEMENTS

Thanks again to everyone at The History Press for making my dreams come true, especially to my commissioning editor, Becky LeJeune, Jaime Muehl and everyone else in production who made me look smart. I would also like to thank the Pikes Peak Library District, especially librarians Jody Jones and Susan, who shared a unique ghostly encounter with me in the Carnegie Building. A huge thanks to retired police detective Dwight Haverkorn, who made my research not only easier but a whole lot of fun as well. I would also like to acknowledge my fourth-grade teacher, Rhoda Wilcox, who inspired me by writing some of the first entertaining history books about the region, and Mrs. Nicks at Coronado High School, who encouraged me to write long before I had a voice. Hats off to the Old Colorado Historical Society and the Fountain Valley Museum, especially to Elaine MacKay and Betty Powell. The people I interviewed deserve a big pat on the back, especially the Cimino and Leasure families, who must have thought it was a joke when they received my letter requesting an interview. A hearty thanks to the SpiritChasers, Christopher Allen Brewer and James Manda, who helped me more than words can say with their wealth of knowledge about the paranormal. The eleventh-hour interview trophy goes to Laszlo Palos, Dorothy Tunnicliff, Robert Rais and Jan Kirk. Special thanks to ghost-hunting friends in Denver and Pueblo, as well as Cripple Creek and Victor. I also want to thank Jana Botello, Wayne Morris, Mike Coletta, Jerry Murphy, Sandy Fitzpatrick, Gail Anne Bailey, Eva Calloway, Sita Ahlen, Hannah Ahlen, Mom, Dad, Tom, Bix, Kameron, Everett, Kristy, in-laws, out-laws, fellow ghost hunters, family, friends, Siddhartha, Mary Jane, monkeys, Wyatt, Jesse, K.K. and the last fish in the sea.

WHY DID I BECOME A GHOST HUNTER?

E very haunting has a ghost and every ghost has a story. I often heard urban legends and ghost tales about spooky places while I was growing up and always wondered what the truth was behind the hauntings. Perhaps that's why I became a paranormal investigator. My interest in ghost hunting began when my folks bought a little farm east of Colorado Springs back in the late 1960s. I remember being so happy when I made a new friend who lived just across the cow pasture. Randy was so darn funny, and he could blow the biggest milk bubbles I had ever seen. One memorable afternoon, we had a strange experience when we went horseback riding at Sand Creek and saw the figure of an Indian warrior that whooped and hollered battle cries as he galloped passed us on his ghostly white steed. We were deathly afraid, but we followed him on our ponies for a while until he slowly faded away.

When I excitedly told my family about the strange ghostly encounter, my southern-born grandmother smiled and said I inherited a psychic gift from her called "the Shine." But my mom blamed my so-called sixth sense on being accidently dropped on the head at birth. Randy's dad didn't believe him either, but at least he didn't give him a lame excuse. His dad just whipped his butt for being a liar and ordered him straight to bed without supper. The supernatural experience at Sand Creek became a catalyst for my early career in ghost hunting, and I formed a strong conviction that we spirit chasers had to stick together. So I started a ghost-hunting club (decades before it was fashionable) and elected myself president. I made

Randy second in command and Grandma Jessie chauffeur. We built a fort by Sand Creek and christened our new enterprise the Sneaky Flats because it sounded cool as well as scary.

One afternoon, Grandma Jessie took the Sneaky Flats on a ghost hunt/picnic at Evergreen Cemetery, and I was really scared because I had never been in a graveyard. However, I didn't want Randy to smell my fear, so I jumped out of the car and hollered like Tarzan as I skipped through the ancient headstones. I was trying to impress Randy with my bravery…then we danced in the water sprinklers until lunchtime. Ghost hunting is hard work, so to replenish our energy we munched on grilled cheese sandwiches and guzzled down root beer. We were having a grand old time competing in an exciting belching contest until I almost lost my lunch—right after Grandma Jessie told us that we were sitting on her uncle's grave! Grandma laughed at my reaction and then introduced us to the rest of the family by pointing out their headstones. Grandma Jessie told us a sad story about her great-great-grandmother, who died in childbirth, and the thought of old grannies giving birth made me laugh so hard that root beer shot out my nose.

After lunch, we walked around the ancient cemetery as Grandma Jessie told us stories about how Colorado Springs began. Our first stop was the headstone of founding father General William Jackson Palmer, who was a Civil War hero and benefactor to the city. Many of Palmer's friends were wealthy British patrons who were a great influence on the upstart town, and it wasn't long before they started calling Colorado Springs "Little London." Palmer came from a conservative Quaker background, so he prohibited the sale or consumption of alcohol within city limits. That's when folks started going to Colorado City to

Early guide to the Pikes Peak region. *Author's collection.*

get their kicks. Colorado City truly was a Wild West town that offered all kinds of lascivious entertainment, including saloons, gambling halls, opium dens and a thriving red-light district. Eventually, the little frontier town of Colorado City became absorbed by Colorado Springs, as did several other little cow towns in the area.

The cover of my first book, *Haunted Manitou Springs.*

Next we saw the gravestone of mining magnate Winfield Scott Stratton, who was the first mega millionaire of the Cripple Creek gold rush. Colorado Springs was fortunate to have had so many generous benefactors, and a lot of them made their fortunes in mining. I thought it was so sad when we saw the graves of all the people who had died of tuberculosis in the early 1900s. Legions of people across the country contracted the horrific disease, and many of them flocked to the dry climate of the Pikes Peak region as a last hope. Hundreds of people in the Colorado Springs area died from the epidemic, and at one time it was said that there were more citizens buried in the cemetery than there were living topside. After the history lesson, we piled in the car and drove around while Grandma Jessie pointed out tourist attractions that distinguished the Pikes Peak Region—like Garden of the Gods, Seven Falls, Cheyenne Mountain Zoo, the Air Force Academy and Manitou Springs. Living on the prairie really made me appreciate the drive up Cheyenne Canyon to beautiful Helen Hunt Falls, and when we got to the top of Gold Camp Road, I could see all the way to Kansas! That day, I decided that I really liked living in Colorado Springs because there was always something exciting to do, and you could easily pretend to be on vacation whenever you wanted.

I still like storytelling, history, adventure and, most of all, ghost hunting. Perhaps that's why I started Blue Moon Haunted History Tours a decade ago and Colorado Ghost Tours LLC a few years later. In 2009, I had a cancer scare that reminded me that there were still a few things I wanted to do before I died. One of the items on my bucket list was to write a book about historical regional ghost stories. Imagine my surprise when The History Press called to ask if I would be interested in writing a book. I knew it would be baptism by fire since I had never done such a thing, but I took a leap of faith anyway, and *Haunted Manitou Springs* was published in 2011. I had so much fun that I begged The History Press to let me write another. Hence, I continued to conduct interviews and spent another year doing research; needless to say, I was in hog heaven (that's something only a true history geek would admit to). Both of my books are rooted in historical fact, and newspaper articles have been included whenever possible. All the haunted locations are public places that have been documented by experienced paranormal investigators, so you won't find any urban legends about a McDonald's in Rockrimmon where the ghost of an Indian chief boils teenagers in the deep fryer! I hope that you will enjoy reading this collection of historical haunted tales and then go on an exciting ghost-hunting adventure of your very own. Happy Hauntings!

THE PHANTOM AXE MAN
OF DEAD MAN'S CANYON

Like one that on a lonesome road
Doth walk in fear and dread,
And having once turned round walks on,
And turns no more his head;
Because he knows a frightful fiend
Doth close behind him tread.
—*Samuel Taylor Coleridge, "The Rime of the Ancient Mariner"*

Dead Man's Canyon is considered to be one of the oldest documented haunted hot spots in the country. Legends of outlaw bandits hiding out in the infamous canyon have flourished for over 150 years. The notorious Espinosa Gang was perhaps the first well-known group of bandits to seek refuge in the canyon's nooks and crannies. Their savage crime spree across the territory caused more fear in the early pioneers, trappers and traders than all the Indian raids combined. The saga of the ruthless gang began in what is now known as New Mexico, where a man named Juan Espinosa lived in his family's ancestral *hacienda* with his large extended family. The clan of ranchers claimed to have Castilian blue blood coursing through their veins and to have descended from the nobles in Cortez's army. The Espinosas also belonged to a mysterious religious cult known as the Penitents, a barbaric sect that practiced bizarre secretive rituals and fanatical violence.

Juan Espinosa was the oldest son and had a fierce hunger for violence. After the Mexican War, some ex–American soldiers went to work on the

Espinosa ranch. One of these men fell in love with Juan's seventeen-year-old sister, and soon they became engaged despite the family's disapproval. The American worked hard and saved a large sum of money in preparation to build a home for his future bride. Juan Espinosa knew that the American hid his savings under his pillow, and he planned to steal it the first chance he got. One late night, the greedy thief crept into the American's dark bedroom hoping to steal his guarded treasure. The American fired his gun but missed, and Juan Espinosa stabbed the American in the heart. The household was startled by the disturbance, and Juan's sister came running. She cried out in horror when she found her brother holding a bloody knife and her lover dead on the floor. The grisly scene instantly struck her with insanity, and before anyone could intervene, she jumped out the window. In a poetic twist of justice, the woman was also pierced through the heart—on the wrought-iron fence below.

With his sister's suicidal cries still ringing in his ears, the desperado and his youngest nephew fled the scene and headed for the Sangre de Cristo Mountains. Over time, they gathered a few sheepherders and trained them to become a gang of murdering thieves and desperados. Juan Espinosa believed that he was some kind of Mexican avenging angel whose holy mission was to kill every American that crossed his path. He especially hated older white men because he blamed previous generations for the Mexican War. Juan was convinced that all white settlers squatting on their ancient Mexican lands needed to be sacrificed, and to show his conviction, he would pierce every victim in the heart and dedicate the victory to the Virgin Mary.

The Espinosa Gang spilled blood all over the region, robbing stagecoaches, wagon trains and Mexican ranches. The hell-bent desperados became known as the "Bloody Espinosa Gang," and their ruthless reign of terror lasted for several years, until greed forced them to leave the motherland. The gang moved into the Pikes Peak region in March 1863, and it didn't take long for the outlaws to kill their first victim—a hardworking sixty-eight-year-old carpenter living in the hills near Cañon City. His lifeless body was found facedown in Hardscrabble Creek with a bullet-riddled heart. The only other clue was a note signed in blood posted to a nearby tree declaring Mexico's independence and the gang's devotion to the Virgin Mary.

The terrorists fled thirty miles to a canyon near Colorado Springs, then known as Sawmill Gulch. The remote area was the perfect outlaw hideout for the notorious Mexican gang, with towering blood red cliffs and plenty of caves, crooks and crannies—all with a bird's-eye view. A few days' rest was all the men needed before killing fifty-five-year-old Henry Harkin in cold blood on the afternoon of March 19, 1863. The old man had just finished chinking the sides of his cabin and was wiping the sweat from his brow when he looked up to see the steely eyed Mexican desperados staring at him from the rocky ridge above. Suddenly, the bandits charged down the hillside and shot Harkin's dog and only horse. The drunken banditos laughed at the horrified Harkins and then danced and sang songs of the Mexican Revolution while shooting their six-guns at everything in sight. The old man watched helplessly as the bandits mocked him with feigned terror and then burned down his barn and tortured him in every way known to mankind. When he finally begged for mercy, they shot him in the heart, split his head with an axe and left the blade hinged in his forehead. After their mission was accomplished, they stole the old man's money and headed for their hideout in the blood red cliffs above.

A few days later, the Espinosa Gang swept through Colorado City, robbing and torturing a seventy-year-old rancher and shooting him through the heart. They killed two additional old men at the train station in Divide and then charged on to Custer County and South Park. They waylaid cabins, stage roads and mining camps, murdering ruthlessly and at whim. The cavalry was even sent to hunt them down, but the Mexican banditos eluded them for months. Finally, Juan Espinosa and his nephew were killed in a hailstorm of bullets just outside Fort Garland. For proof of his assassination, Juan Espinosa's corpse was beheaded, and his noggin was pickled in a jar and sent to the state capitol. The nefarious Espinosa Gang ruthlessly murdered countless victims all over the territory, and the bandits' bloody rampage spun many legends. However, out of all the tales told about the notorious outlaws, the ghost stories about Dead Man's Canyon are the most amazing.

Mr. J.P. Galloway was one of the first to witness the horrifying ghost of Henry Harkin. He was traveling alone through Sawmill Gulch shortly after the murder spree and claimed to see a transparent apparition floating over the trees and bushes beside him. Suddenly, he realized that the ghost had a hatchet stuck in its head and looked just like his old pal Henry Harkin. Galloway screamed for help and then fired his six-shooters, but the menace just laughed and darted about, making his horse buck him right out of the saddle. Denver businessmen Lawrence Poole and Adam T. Baker were traveling slowly behind Galloway but came rushing after hearing his cries for help. The men found the old man cowering behind some rocks, out of breath and out of bullets. The businessmen started shooting at the phantom, but the bullets passed right through him and ricocheted off rocks and the canyon walls. Old man Galloway swung at the paranormal bully with his fists, but the maneuver knocked him off balance and sent him tumbling downhill. The phantom again laughed with wicked abandon and then floated away over the hilltops, leaving Galloway bloodied and dazed.

The businessmen rushed Galloway to Colorado Springs and sought out a physician. When the old man started babbling about being attacked by the ghost of Henry Harkin, the doctor thought Galloway was delusional from his head injury. But when both Poole and Baker confirmed the account, the physician was rendered speechless. The strange story was related all around the country, and folks began to fear going through Sawmill Gulch. It was about this time that pioneers started calling the spooky area Phantom's Canyon, but since that name was already taken by a haunted canyon near Victor, they decided to refer to it as Dead Man's Canyon instead. Sadly, the menacing name has stuck ever since.

One of the most fascinating ghost stories about Dead Man's Canyon began in 1867, when Oliver Kimball went to build a home there for his future wife, Gertrude Osborn. After several months, the young woman grew concerned after not hearing from her fiancé. Fearing the worst, she sent a note to a mutual friend, Captain Marshall Felch in Denver. A few days later, Captain Felch went to Dead Man's Canyon to look for Kimball. While he was setting up camp, he smelled the curious odor of rotten flesh in the wind. He had heard the frightening ghost stories about the area but did not believe in superstitious nonsense. After dinner, he was smoking his corncob pipe and gazing up at the clear night sky when he saw a beautiful white stallion grazing on the grassy knoll above his camp. He excitedly leapt on his horse to try and catch the steed, but it ran over the ridge. The captain made chase, but as he galloped faster, the white horse gained speed, and when he slowed down, the mysterious creature followed suit. So, Felch followed the stallion at a comfortable distance, and after a few minutes it led him to the old Henry Harkins homestead. The captain couldn't believe his eyes when he saw the transparent form of old man Harkin and his dog walking out of his former cabin. Then with a flash, the ghostly figure jumped onto the horse and, followed by his canine companion, charged up the hillside, beckoning Felch to follow.

When the ghostly trio got to the top of the ridge, it disappeared. Then a new phantom emerged from behind a huge boulder looking remarkably like his friend Oliver Kimball. The ghostly figure was attacked by another phantom, and the paranormal beings duked it out until one of them plunged a knife into the other—then the illusion disappeared. Captain Felch rubbed his eyes and looked around for the mysterious apparitions, but the night was still, and the only sound was the wind mocking him in laughter. The next morning, Captain Felch and a nearby rancher went to investigate the area where he had the mystical vision. When they got to the ridge, the captain spied a skeletal hand under some rocks and uncovered the corpse of Oliver Kimball.

Sadly, Gertrude Osborn died the night that Captain Felch found Kimball's grave. The letter from her mother stated that she died of pneumonia, and her last words were: "At last, my darling Oliver has been found, I shall be joining him now." The tragic story propelled Felch to want to find the murderer, so on a hunch he went to the mining camp of California Gulch looking for answers. While sitting around the campfire that night, he told the men how he had found their co-worker Oliver Kimball buried under some rocks with a knife still plunged in his corpse. The miners gasped when Captain Felch pulled the murder weapon from his satchel. The eight-inch steel blade flashed in the firelight as he read the initials engraved on the blade: D.G. The next morning, David Griffin was found dead; his suicide note claimed that he "bit the bullet" because of guilt, and then he confessed to murdering Oliver Kimball. Amazing as it may sound, the ghost of Henry Harkin helped solve the despicable crime, and the phenomenal ghost story was published in newspapers across the country.

A funny story about the menacing phantom of Dead Man's Canyon was published in the *Rocky Mountain* newspaper in July 1884. It told of how Mrs. Clark Wyatt of Colorado Springs and her grandson were driving their one-horse buggy through Dead Man's Canyon when the ghost of Henry Harkin jumped out from a rock and scared them. Mrs. Wyatt cursed the ghost and smacked him with her umbrella. Twenty years earlier, a series of burley bullwhackers and tough muleskinners constantly relayed stories of being chased by the ghost of Henry Harkin; he sometimes followed them all the way to Canyon City and Pueblo. The gruesome-looking ghost of Henry Harkin was sometimes seen riding on his white steed and other times just standing above a cliff staring down at trespassers, but he always had an axe hanging out of his split forehead.

Seasoned ghost hunters have been making pilgrimages to Henry Harkin's grave for over a century. On any given day, you can trek up the hillside and find coins lying on Harkin's old tombstone. Legend says that if you pay Harkin a visit, you have to give him a coin; if you don't, he will haunt

Ghost orbs flying over Henry Harkin's grave. *Courtesy of Wesley Waters.*

your dreams until you do. Colorado Mesa University student Wesley Waters thought he was being clever when he pulled a bloody bandage from his foot after a backpacking expedition and stuck it on Harkin's headstone. His friends warned him about the vengeful ghost and beseeched him to leave a coin instead, but he laughed off their silly warnings. I interviewed Waters about the strange experience, and he said:

> *I couldn't believe my bad luck. For weeks all kinds of strange things happened. Then I remembered the stupid bandage that I stuck on Harkin's grave and wondered if I was being haunted by his pissed-off ghost! The next weekend, I drove the six hours to Dead Man's Canyon, peeled the bloody bandage off Harkin's tombstone and left him a nickel instead. Then I had to drive all the way back home, but the twelve hours on the road were well worth it because I have slept like a baby ever since. I'm still not sure if I believe in ghosts or not, but I do know that it was a surreal experience.*

There really is a dead man in Dead Man's Canyon. The grave of Henry Harkin is south of Colorado Springs on Highway 115. Drive past Fort Carson's main gate and continue driving four miles beyond the fifty-foot-tall, razor-jawed beetle that guards the turnoff to May's Bug Museum. You can park your car at the corner of Highway 115 and Calle de Fuentes Road. Directly across the highway, you will see a white split-rail fence on the top of a knoll. If you pay Harkin a visit, toss him a coin; if you don't, you may be sorry!

HELL HOUNDS OF THE
OLD NORTH END

*Lizzie Borden took an axe and gave her father forty whacks. When she saw what
she had done she gave her mother forty-one.*
—Unknown

Anyone who has ever skipped rope in a schoolyard can recall the haunting nursery rhyme about Lizzie Borden and her hatchet-wielding ways. On August 4, 1892, sixty-five-year-old Andrew Borden lay down for a nap in the parlor of his Victorian mansion in Fall River, Massachusetts, unaware as he drifted off to sleep that his rest would be eternal. Police discovered his axe-battered corpse in the parlor and then found Mrs. Borden in an upstairs bedroom, also beaten beyond repair. Newspapers across the country speculated that Lizzie had blood on her hands even though she was tried and acquitted of the crimes. The spinster was ostracized from society, and even her sizeable inheritance was not enough to shelter her from loneliness. She died from pneumonia thirty-five long, miserable years later, still vehemently maintaining her innocence until the end. The infamous murder case was never cracked, and Lizzie Borden became a notorious figure in American folklore.

After the Borden tragedy, a series of twenty-five copycat axe murders erupted across the country. Hardest hit were the states of Illinois, Missouri, Iowa and Kansas. Interestingly enough, a rancher in Ohio admitted to brutally beating "a couple of cows" with an axe and received a life sentence because one of the victims happened to be his mother-in-law. Although these crimes were certainly heinous, none could be compared to the gruesome murders that occurred in the city of Colorado Springs a century ago. The infamous murders happened in September 1911 and left an indelible scar on the community. Old-timers still recall the horrific month of terror with a shudder. Few things were scarier back in the olden times than an axe-wielding maniac running amok in your backyard, and the haunting that resulted from the murderous attacks became legendary.

The old north end neighborhood surrounds the so-called Ivy League campus of Colorado College. It is one of the oldest neighborhoods in town and is often described as Rockwell-esque, with its wide avenues canopied by ancient oak trees. Stone walls and scrolled iron fences lace between blue-collar cottage homes and the historic mansions of bluebloods. Even small homes in this desirable part of town are sold at premium prices. That's why it's hard to imagine a large double lot in this neighborhood sitting vacant for over a century as it has, but it wasn't always that way. The vacant lot on Dale Street once had two identical cottages surrounded by a large splendid garden where children laughed and played. Now, all that remains are memories of a tragedy that happened there long ago and the ghosts that were left behind.

The horrors began when scores of dead canines started to litter the city streets and sidewalks around Colorado College. At first, it seemed to be just unwanted strays; however, police became alarmed when it appeared that the hapless hounds had eaten poisoned meat. Strychnine had been placed on pieces of sausage and scattered in ditches and alleys throughout the north end neighborhood. Days later, several beloved pets on prestigious Wood Avenue fell victim to the cruelty, including Ballou, the shepherd-collie mix owned by the Colorado College dean of students. Tension in the community mounted, especially after the *Colorado Springs Gazette* headlined a story about another brutal dog poisoning just down the street:

SLICK IS DEAD

HIGH SCHOOL TERRORS' MASCOT DOG POISONED—PLAYERS ON WARPATH FOR MISCREANT

"Slick,'" a common everyday dog of unusual fighting ability and mascot for the High School Terrors during the last two football seasons, is dead. Every high school football player is on the warpath, for "Slick" was poisoned Monday afternoon. If the poisoner is found, what the Terrors will do to him will be "plenty."

Slick was found viciously growling with blood frothing from his mouth shortly after eating a sausage found on the high school football field. Upon encountering the crazed animal, one player yelled, "Mad dog!" and teammates jumped for the safety of the bleachers. Moments later, Slick fell dead in his tracks, an obvious victim of poison.

A few bystanders claimed to have heard the bell of a butcher's wagon just before witnessing a man throwing sausages over the fence. They claimed the tall, skinny Italian seemed crazy because he laughed maniacally before driving away. Moments later, the beloved mascot experienced a short but agonizing death. Witnesses to the horrific assault were relieved that at least it didn't take long for Slick to pass over the Rainbow Bridge.

Newspapers warned citizens that a maniacal Italian butcher was in their midst, wantonly poisoning animals with careless abandon and law enforcement cautioned citizens to keep a careful eye on their pets. Apparently, the Burnham family did not heed the warnings because their mutt was poisoned, and the rotting canine remained unburied in their front yard for days. That's when neighbors noticed that a hush had fallen over the twin cottage homes of the Burnham and Wayne families. The silence seemed suspicious considering that young children lived in each household. The Wayne family was new to town, having just arrived from Indiana a few weeks earlier. Mr. Wayne was a tuberculosis patient, as was Mr. Burnham, who lived next door. The two young clans had several things in common and might have become good friends, but fate intervened and that day never came.

Mrs. Nettie Ruth was concerned about her pregnant sister, Alice, so she secured a passkey and nervously walked to the Burnham home unsure of what she might find. A foul stench rushed to greet her as she opened the back door. A few unwashed dishes remained in the sink, and last week's newspaper was neatly folded on the table. She surmised that the Burnhams' parrot had died and caused the foul stench that permeated the home. Nettie continued down the hallway, lifted the latch over the door and entered the dark bedroom, gagging as the putrid odor grew almost unbearable. Suddenly, the loud-mouthed parrot startled her when it squawked: "END OF THE LINE... DAMN YOUR SOUL...HAHAHA!"

She ignored the flippant bird's macabre warning and stumbled into the dark room to open the curtains. Sunlight revealed cream-colored walls splattered with dark-colored blotches. On the bed, she saw a pile of muddied clothes...and her sister's crushed skull resting on a crusty brown pillow. Two little children were tucked in bed beside her, and all three of their heads were beaten beyond recognition. One of the toddlers appeared to have awakened during the horrific assault and tried to escape; her tiny torso hung over the side of the mattress like a wilted flower.

Across the street at the Collins Grocery Store, only two telephone calls were made—one to the police and one to the coroner. However, the news spread like wildfire, and by the time deputies arrived, the whole community had gathered to see what the commotion was about; everyone, that is, except the Wayne family.

Drawn by suspicion, police burst through the back door of the Wayne home. In the bedroom, as if asleep, the young family lay tucked in bed—mother, father and baby covered in a blanket of blood and splattered brains. A bloodstained axe found near the cottages was no doubt the murder weapon. Friends and neighbors were interviewed when the officers arrived to investigate. All accounts told of how both families were welcome additions to the neighborhood, and no known enemies were found. The state of decay of the corpses indicated that the butchery had happened several days earlier. The fact that such a brutal crime could have happened unnoticed in a quiet neighborhood caused great alarm. Even more puzzling was that robbery did not appear to be a motive; both women were still wearing their wedding rings, and Mr. Wayne's gold pocket watch was lying in plain view on the dresser.

Forty-two-year-old Arthur James Burnham was the only family member spared from the horrible tragedy. Burnham was a resident patient of the Woodman tuberculosis sanatorium outside town, and he told investigators that he had not left the hospital property in over a week. The quiet tuberculosis patient did not seem like a ruthless killer; nevertheless, he was forcibly taken to the crime scene, despite his protests of not wanting to step foot inside the "house of slaughter." When Mr. Burnham begrudgingly opened the door to his bedroom, the unruly parrot greeted him with the same rigmarole: "END OF THE LINE…DAMN YOUR SOUL…HAHAHA!"

Stunned by the outburst of the foul-mouthed bird, Burnham fell to the floor murmuring cries of disbelief that anything so terrible could have happened to his beloved family. Although police did not seriously suspect he was the perpetrator, they arrested and held him in jail anyway because he was the only viable suspect that they had. City leaders tried desperately to keep the news from hitting the press. The fact that a serial-killing, axe-wielding maniac was at large was enough to start a ruckus of enormous proportions. But it was too late. News of the hideous crime slapped citizens smack dab in the face when newspaper boys screamed from every street corner:

Extra! Extra! Read all about it! Wanton axe murderer raids Colorado Springs…Still at large…Wholesale murderer kills while victims lay sleeping…Two whole families almost completely annihilated!

Fear strangled the city, and many old-timers later told how the panic of that day was even worse than the Indian Raids of 1864. Sheriff George Birdsell and county commissioner Harry Hutchinson agreed that in desperate times one needed to employ desperate measures. The men were given carte blanche by the mayor of Colorado Springs to hire Pinkerton's best detectives. Special posses of eight armed and mounted skilled trackers were organized to scour the hillsides in hope of finding the axe-wielding maniac.

A few days later, the bodies of the Wayne family were shipped back to their home in Indiana for burial, while the Burnhams were laid to rest in Evergreen Cemetery. The Burnham family funeral brought out a crowd of five hundred mourners, and Arthur Burnham was allowed to attend the service under police supervision. The heartbroken victim sobbed uncontrollably over the three coffins, his frail body shaking as he proclaimed, "By God, I am innocent. I am innocent, I tell you!"

Detectives became convinced of Burnham's innocence, and the widower was released from custody and sent back to the sanatorium. However, the tuberculosis patient died just two months later, a victim of the disease that had brought him to Colorado Springs five years earlier. He was buried in Evergreen Cemetery next to the fresh graves of his wife and children.

After Burnham's death, forty-one-year-old bachelor Anthony Donatello became the investigator's newest suspect. Acquaintances claimed that the tall, skinny Italian had carried a torch for the pregnant mother of two even though she was happily married to Burnham. Donatello was arrested because some believed the Italian stallion was jealous of Mr. Burnham and wanted him dead. Police acted on the wild theory that Donatello accidently killed the Wayne family, realized his mistake and then went next door looking for Mr. Burnham, killing Mrs. Burnham and her children instead. While in jail, Donatello seemed unfazed when asked about his relationship with Mrs. Burnham and admitted only to being her friend. The swarthy Italian calmly smoked his corncob pipe while being interviewed and confessed to being a landlord and butcher by trade. He admitted to occasionally killing stray dogs for their exotic-tasting meat and boasted that some breeds—like poodles, for example—tasted simply delightful in Italian sausage. The proud Italian even offered samples to reporters, bragging about his great-grandmother's secret

Sicilian recipe. The landlord/butcher denied exaggerated stories about his violent temper, even though it was well known that just a few weeks earlier he had been slapped with a fine for assaulting a neighbor boy. Donatello confirmed that he was evicted from his homeland of Italy when he was a young man because of his temper. Stories about the immigrant getting angry and biting off his own brother's ear were also verified. Then Donatello politely concluded the jaw dropping interview by saying that he was no guiltier of committing the Dale Street murders than were the reporters.

Although there was a lack of evidence, many people believed that Donatello was guilty, and one *Gazette Telegraph* article questioned the Italian's mental stability. Neighbors often told how he feverishly scrubbed the walls of his rental properties, trying to rid evil marks left by demons and witches. After the Dale Street murders, his paranoia grew, and he feared that phantom hounds, as well as angry ghosts, were torturing his mortal soul.

Spurred by neighbors, police got a search warrant and went to Donatello's home in hot pursuit of evidence. However, all their training and experience never could have prepared them for what they were about to see next. When they opened the wooden gate to Donatello's backyard, detectives were confronted with the biggest boneyard they had ever seen. Piles and piles of shattered skeletal remains of every shape and size littered the lot, and the menagerie was so large that it nearly spilled over the fence. However, the recent signs of slaughter were the most unsettling; the stench of soured blood hung in the still night air, and the ground was so saturated with blood that it squished as the policemen pensively walked to the door. When officers entered the shack, they were astonished to find that the miser insulated his home by using dog hides. Dozens upon dozens of tanned furs from Dalmatians to wiener dogs upholstered the inside walls of the shabby hut. The smoking gun they were looking for was buried under the bed—a leather satchel stuffed with what looked like bloodstained clothes. However, all hopes of solving the unthinkable crimes were dashed when lab tests revealed that the supposed bloodstains were nothing but dried spaghetti sauce.

Desperately seeking answers, the investigators made a last-ditch effort to crack the case by hiring a well-known psychic, but even she had difficulty reading the case. Police knew that it was the end of the line for the murder investigation when they realized that the only witness to the horrific tragedy was a foul-mouthed parrot with a limited vocabulary. Regrettably, police were forced to release Anthony Donatello from custody even though they had a hunch that the Italian was the man they were looking for. Though exonerated of the crimes, suspicion followed Donatello for the rest of his

Strange light coming from a haunted old north end home. *Courtesy of Colorado Ghost Tours LLC.*

days. Ironically, he was ostracized from society and died sick and alone many years later, just like Lizzie Borden.

A ghost story was born when neighbors began to complain about the sound of dogs howling and horrible cries for help coming from the vacant cottages on Dale Street. Finally, a group of concerned citizens banded together and marched to city hall, demanding that the evil twin cottages be destroyed. Colorado Springs officials agreed that razing the homes on the dead-end street was the best way to rid the property of the ghosts and sweep away the unsavory memories of the unsolved murders. Years later, many people believe that the old north end neighborhood near the Dale Street murders is extremely haunted. Voices can still be heard shrieking for help at all hours of the night, and the complaints have become so common that police rarely respond anymore.

Yet another frightening nuisance is the presence of spectral hounds that howl a plaintive wail on full moon nights. Old north-enders have come to call them the "hounds from hell" and believe that they are evil spirits hunting the souls of the dead. One of the believers is an old-timer by the name of Eva Calloway, who grew up on Yampa Street. Eva collaborated with me for this story and has lived near the murder site for over seventy years. She and others have witnessed dozens of paranormal apparitions at night wandering through the neighborhood, always accompanied by a litany of invisible barking hounds. She firmly believes it is because of the axe murders that happened there long ago and said, "There just ain't no way you can get rid of something like that because the murders have gone unavenged!"

Eva finds it ironic that the old north end neighborhood has found a particular niche when it comes to decorating for Halloween. A majority of the historic homes feature elaborately decorated lawns with traditional jack-o'-lanterns, skeletons and mock cemetery scenes. However, some of the more menacing yards depict gruesome-looking axe-wielding mannequins. She finds it strange and tasteless but admits that even she has a secret fascination for the macabre. Many citizens of Colorado Springs have all but forgotten the haunting tale of the old north end axe murders, so Eva was delighted to have the chance to share her memories of the ghost story as told by her mother long ago. She concluded the interview by quipping, "It's getting late, and I have to get to bed now…It's the end of the line for this old lady…Hahaha!"

THE RIDDLE AND WRAITH
OF CHEYENNE CANYON

What beck'ning ghost, along the moonlight shade
Invites my step, and points to yonder glade?
—*Alexander Pope, "Elegy to the Memory of an Unfortunate Young Lady"*

Cheyenne Mountain was the subject of several spooky Indian legends long before the French and Spaniards explored the region. One legend told that the mountain was once a gigantic thirsty lizard that drank all the water that once covered the earth. Another explained that an Indian god named Manitou took the devil to Cheyenne Mountain and threw him into the canyon with his head facing the heavens; the Devil's Horns (a rock formation) can still be seen there to this day.

General Palmer thought Cheyenne Canyon was so beautiful that he wanted to share it with all the citizens of Colorado Springs. So he purchased the property with his associate, Dr. Fred Chamberlain, and gifted it to the city in 1885. The ancient canyon is known for its towering lodgepole pines, stunning wildflowers, rock formations, breathtaking views and waterfalls. Helen Hunt Falls was named in honor of American writer and Colorado Springs resident Helen Hunt Jackson. The famous author dedicated her life to Indian reform and was buried at a lookout point on Cheyenne Mountain just above her namesake waterfall. The ancient canyon also has a couple old dirt stagecoach trails that lace through it. The roads are still used by anyone who wants a bird's-eye view of Colorado Springs and the eastern plains. Years ago, the bones of

An antique postcard of Helen Hunt Falls. *Author's collection.*

a cheating gambler were discovered stuffed in some rocks above Old Stage Road. Occasionally, human skeletal remains are still found in the crooks, crannies and caves, lending credence to urban legends about the area being a body dump ever since the days of the Wild West.

Old Stage Road was taken over by the railroad during the Cripple Creek gold rush, and legends of Tommyknockers haunting the old tunnels became popular. Tommyknockers are said to be the ghosts of dead miners. These legendary spirits were known to make a knocking noise to warn of impending danger in mines and railroad tunnels. In the last century, a popular urban legend says that a school bus filled with youngsters stalled in tunnel number three. The selfish driver immediately evacuated when he heard the train whistling down the track. Tragically, every child was killed when the school bus was annihilated by a passing train. Local lore claims that after driving through the ancient passageway, tiny handprints can be seen on your vehicle. There is no question that the old tunnels are haunted; however, it is doubtful that they are inhabited by ghosts of grammar school kids with sticky fingers. The rails were pulled off the road long ago, when school buses were still just a vision of the future.

Another well-known ghost story about the infamous area is known as "The Riddle of Alex Riddle." Riddle's gruesome ghost has been seen in Cheyenne Canyon for over a century. The story goes that in late November 1904, a tourist took the trolley from downtown Colorado Springs to the Stratton Park Depot near the entrance of Cheyenne Canyon. However, when the confused tourist got off the train, he thought he was in the town of Trinidad and spent the afternoon looking for his ride home from the station. A few days later, Miss Flora Staub was horrified to stumble across the corpse of the dead stranger on the hillside. Detectives were called, and his identity was established as Alex Riddle from Trinidad, Colorado.

An antique tourist guide photo of haunted Gold Camp Road tunnels. *Author's collection.*

Authorities reasoned that the victim had an epileptic fit and then died from exposure. "Exposure" was an interesting choice of words, since Mr. Riddle was found *very exposed*. His body was found stripped of not only his clothes but all his skin as well! Alex Riddle was said to be a handsome man, but that would have been difficult to determine since his head was also missing. Detectives were mystified as to why and how the corpse had been mutilated. A posse of men on horseback took to the hills in search of clues, but when none was found, the case was closed. However, six years later, when the Cheyenne Canon Inn was built on the exact spot where Alex Riddle's mutilated corpse was found, guests at the upscale hotel began complaining about seeing a headless, skinless man walking outside their windows at night. Innkeepers were mystified about who the ghost could possibly be until an old newspaper article surfaced about Alex Riddle's mysterious death. Legend says that the fleshless haunt can still be seen around the Cheyenne Canon Inn to this very day.

Oddly enough, in 1904, another naked tourist was found dead in the canyon, and her death also resulted in an infamous haunting. The mysterious murder on Mount Cutler inspired national headlines and kept its audience of armchair detectives spellbound while law enforcement across the country tried to hunt down the wealthy globetrotting suspects. Criminal buffs still recall the fascinating murder case because it was one of the first situations were forensic science was used to identify a victim. Ghost hunters are familiar with the story because of the phenomenal haunting that resulted after the murder. The menacing ghost on Mount Cutler hides among the trees and startles hikers with a haunting shriek before disappearing with a flash of light. A few backpackers and rock climbers over the years have been so frightened by the wraith's attack that they have slipped from the trail and fallen to their deaths. The frightening apparition has been seen for over one hundred years and has since become known as the "Wraith of Mount Cutler."

The story begins in August 1904, when young, beautiful socialite Bessie Kempter checked into the Antlers Hotel alone. However, she was soon seen palling around with a deplorable-looking stranger who drew considerable attention because he seemed an unsuitable match for the sophisticated heiress. The mysterious man was at least ten years older and stood a good foot taller than Bessie. He looked emaciated, and his pasty complexion was often damp with perspiration. The oddest thing about the man was that he always wore a black wool cape, regardless of the season. The sinister-looking garment was obviously worn to hide a ghoulish birth defect: a deformed, shallow chest. This unusual affliction caused him great pain, and he always carried an arsenal of pills, powders and potions in an old leather hatbox that never left his side.

The odd couple was often seen socializing together, leaving other hotel guests to speculate about their relationship. However, it soon became apparent that they both loved to live the high life and especially enjoyed drinking absinthe, also known as "flying with the green fairy." The expensive chartreuse-colored liquor was a favorite indulgence of the couple, as it was known to have hallucinogenic properties. However, their so-called flights of fancy often led them to make embarrassing public spectacles of themselves.

One night, Bessie tossed the hatbox out the window because she believed her companion had laced her absinthe with poisoned sugar cubes. An explosive argument ensued after Bessie threw a crystal decanter at her companion's head and the doctor was called to stitch the gash. The resulting souvenir of the potshot was a garish purple scar that stretched from the man's left ear to his chin. The next morning, the star-crossed lovers checked out of the hotel—separately. One guest commented that Bessie and her mysterious companion both lived hard and played hard and would likely die hard, as well; she ruefully added, "If you play with fire, then you're going to get burned!" Little did she know at the time how true her dismal prediction would become.

A few months later, Dr. Chamberlain and his neighbor were hiking to the summit of Mount Cutler when they were startled to see a nude woman sunbathing on some fallen logs. However, as they approached, it slowly dawned on them that the naked woman was dead. Her head had been braced between two logs, resting facedown just inches above a fire pit where a few cold embers still remained. The victim's skin was charred, and her vacant eyes were devoid of color. An empty bottle of poison lay nearby, and a small-caliber bullet was lodged in her skull. Chamberlain surmised that the woman had been poisoned and then taken to the remote location and shot. Afterward, she was stripped, and her face was placed over a fire pit to conceal her identity. He reasoned that she had been dead for a while and that the cold, dry climate had kept her body from decomposing. Lawmen were notified, and the hillsides were scoured for any possible clues, but nothing was found—not a coat, hat or shoe. It was as if the mystery woman had dropped naked from the clear blue sky.

The horrific story seemed to profoundly affect all who heard about it, and the fact that the baffling mystery happened just before Christmas made the case seem even more macabre. Dr. Chamberlain took a particular interest in the case and placed ads in big-city newspapers advertising a $1,000 reward for any information while the corpse was kept on ice in the city morgue. Three weeks later, Coroner Law demanded that the unknown woman be given a decent Christian burial, and several hundred sympathetic citizens attended the service in paupers' field. A sadder funeral there surely never was, and the *Colorado Springs Gazette Telegraph* even noted so in its Christmas Day edition.

One night, Chief Detective Reynolds had a lucid dream about the faceless victim. She appeared to him as a dark shadow flying through treetops and calling his name between tearful moans and pitiful sobs. He awoke with a startle and, in a flash, got an ingenious idea about how to identify the corpse. It was easier than he expected getting a court order to have the victim's body exhumed. Coroner Law made a graphic account of the unusual amount of costly dental work and a corresponding chart with a full description of the gold-capped teeth and bridgework of the victim. Then he methodically copied and mailed ten thousand circulars and sent them to police departments and dentist offices across the country. Fortunately, the tactic worked, and it didn't take long for Dr. Isaac Burton of nearby Denver to respond. The older physician was about to retire, so it was a miracle when he happened upon the flyer and was able to identify the dental work as belonging to Mrs. Bessie Kempter Bouton from Syracuse, New York.

Police interviewed Mr. George Bouton in Syracuse about his young wife and learned that the last time he had heard from her was on October 7, when she sent a postcard saying to set an extra place at the table because she would be home for Thanksgiving. But Thanksgiving came and went without a word from Bessie. Mr. Bouton was distraught, although not surprised, after learning about Bessie's murder. The older gentleman told investigators that he was aware of her independent, carefree lifestyle and feared that it might get her into trouble someday.

Once Colorado Springs detectives had a name for their victim, they started looking for the perpetrator. Police sketches of Bessie and of the mystery man last seen with her were drawn up and scattered throughout the country. Fortunately, a break in the case came when a clerk at a drugstore near the Broadmoor recognized a police sketch of Bessie's creepy companion as a man who had picked up his prescriptions under the name of Mr. Milton Franklin Andrews. Through his trusty police work, Detective Reynolds learned that Andrews was a traveling con artist known as "Long Shot" Andrews, but from there the case went cold. Two years went by, and authorities feared that the case would never be solved. Then, out of the blue, some startling news came from San Francisco in July 1906.

The police report indicated that Andrews and his girlfriend had just returned from Australia two days prior. The team of con artists met a wealthy horseman by the name of William Ellis on their passage back from Australia and invited him to dinner. Just before dessert, Andrews robbed Ellis and whipped him with a pistol. The dazed businessman woke up in a closet an hour later and overheard the couple arguing about how to dismember his body. Fortunately, Mr. Ellis was able to escape his captors by climbing out the window. Police arrived just moments later to find Andrews and his redheaded lover lying dead in a pool of blood. A suicide note written by Andrews denied any involvement in the murder of Bessie even though her diamond-encrusted Tiffany watch was found on the dead woman lying next to him. It was revealed that, like Bessie Kempter Bouton, Andrew Franklin Milton also had a secret life. His suicide note instructed authorities to ship his remains to his wife and ten-year-old son living in Holyoke, Massachusetts.

Over one hundred years later, armchair detectives still wonder if Bessie was murdered not just for her money but also because she knew too much about Andrew Franklin Milton; many people now believe that Milton was actually an author who went by the pen name S.W. Erandise. Erandise wrote an infamous book in 1902 called *The Expert and the Card Table*, the bible for sleight-of-hand and cheating techniques. Could S.W. Erandise be an anagram for Andrew Franklin Milton? Would Andrews kill to keep a secret? How could Andrews have killed Bessie Kempter Bouton if he was in Australia? These questions will likely never be answered, as the gambler played his last hand and took his greatest secret to his grave.

Old timers will tell you that Mount Cutler has been haunted ever since the nefarious murder happened there long ago. The haunting was first recounted by a man named John Stone, who lived nearby the murder scene. His bone-chilling story was published in the *Gazette Telegraph* on November 11, 1906:

> *There is a place on Cutler Mountain, where wintry winds sweep fallen leaves and sighing pines, a shadow lurks, the lowing form and phantom face of a woman. Her long hair streams in the wind and she glides among the crags and the trees. She's quiet only a moment, and then with a shriek she fades into nothingness. Is the wraith like creature Bessie Bouton?*
>
> *John Stone who resides near bear creek canyon says it is. He saw the ghost on Sunday night, coming from the trees…The apparition hovers around the spot where the body of Bessie Bouton was found, with a bullet in her brain and her face burnt to a crisp to prevent identification. Stone said that he felt a peculiar rush of cold air and then a figure uttered a shriek and vanished. Stone began to reason that perhaps the elusive form was that of a woman who had become lost in the mountains and had gone insane from suffering. He called aloud; the only answer was the echo of his voice and the answer of the wind laughing through the branches of the pines. He looked for footprints in the snow which covered the mountainside. There was none except those he made himself…*

The ghost of Bessie has since become known as the "Wraith of Mount Cutler," and her dangerous haunting presence is still felt on the mountain to this very day. As recently as May 13, 2011, college students Kameron Moding and Page Waters hiked to the summit and had a very mysterious experience. Page claimed to have heard someone calling her name like a whisper in the wind. She thought that Kameron was playing a trick on her, but she followed the haunting sound until she was suddenly blinded by a flash of light, heard a deafening scream and then was pushed from behind! Thankfully she recovered her balance before nearly falling from the edge of a five-hundred-foot cliff!

Like a siren's song that lures fishing boats to crash on the rocks, the haunting scream of the wraith has caused many hikers to topple over the cliffs of Mount Cutler. If you decide to hike the infamous scenic trail, take a friend and never under any circumstances should you follow the vindictive call of the wraith—because if you do, you just might join the mystical mistress of the mountain for all eternity.

THE SHADOW BOXER OF
KID MONTANA

The boundaries which divide Life from Death are at best shadowy and vague.
Who shall say where the one ends, and the other begins?
—Edgar Allan Poe

In the 1880s, Colorado Springs was affectionately dubbed "Little London" because many of its earliest residents relocated from across the pond. The British invasion was largely due to the influence of Englishman Dr. William Bell, founding father of Manitou Springs and associate of General Palmers. Residents and tourists alike enjoyed stalwart British customs like slurping down beans for breakfast and sipping afternoon tea. Recreation and sports were also largely influenced by the motherland, as polo, croquet and lawn tennis became popular. By the early 1900s, the archaic sport of boxing had resurged as a popular sport in England, and fascination with the so-called sweet science spread all the way to Little London. World heavyweight boxing champ Jack Dempsey was from Manassa, Colorado, and would often train at Turkey Creek Ranch near southwestern Colorado Springs. The ranch was the breadbasket for the Broadmoor Hotel, and it was owned by Dempsey's friend Spencer Penrose.

Penrose was a big promoter of the sport, and several grand boxing events were hosted in Little London. One memorable event was the world lightweight championship, held on September 4, 1916. The sold-out tournament matched America's Charles White against champion Freddy Welsh from England. Thousands of people came from all over the world to attend. Bets were placed, and fortunes were lost and won as buckets of blood were spilled. The third round was especially brutal when a section of makeshift bleachers near Colorado and Spruce Streets collapsed, and five hundred people crashed to the ground. Tragically, one hundred of them had to be hospitalized, and three people died. However, there's nothing like bloodshed to excite a crowd, and the fight went on for seven more thunderous rounds until Welsh conquered White in an unmatched victory.

Former middleweight champion David Reese was at the fight that afternoon and bragged that he could have taken the title when he was in top form. He often told how his love for fighting began at a young age because his drunken father bullied him into learning self-defense. He ran away from home when he was still wet behind the ears and ended up in Montana doing odd jobs like shining shoes and hawking newspapers. The boy learned life's lessons from the school of hard knocks and then returned home a few years later with revenge in his heart and a left hook that could drop a man twice his size. David's first order of business was to set the record straight with his old man, and when word of the knockout got around, folks started calling him the "Comeback Kid." The cocky young whippersnapper would boldly swagger into the saloons and announce, "I can't dance and I can't sing, but I bet any SOB in here that I could whip them in the boxing ring!" In the beginning, several men stepped up to take the teenager's challenge, and the kid whipped them without even breaking a sweat. It didn't take long for David to earn a feared reputation because few of his opponents ever left the match on their own accord; most were taken out by stretcher.

One night, after an especially impressive battle of fisticuffs, a professional ex-boxer offered to train the Comeback Kid in the sweet science and make him a legitimate prizefighter. The aspiring athlete jumped at the opportunity and worked hard by training regularly at the local YMCA. Within a year, he was competing in some of the finest fight clubs in the country and became known as "Kid Montana." The good-looking brawny Irishman with the magnetic smile was admired by women wherever he went. However, the Kid soon caved to the affections of a young woman named Grace Frank, who came all the way from Kansas to watch him fight in Cripple Creek. Three days later, David and Grace were married at the Teller County Courthouse. David was said to be over the moon when his first child, William, was born nine months later. The boy was soon followed by sister Lorena and brother David. They bought a home in Colorado City, and David traveled the country making a decent living as a prizefighter.

A few years later, a Colorado Avenue trolley accident changed the champ's life forever. A transmitter caused a mild explosion, and David jumped from the moving car. Doctors at Bethel Hospital admonished the champ for the reckless maneuver and told him he was lucky that he didn't get killed. However, David saw himself as a victim and sued the Transcontinental Train Company. The lengthy lawsuit sought compensation for bodily pain, mental anguish and lost income. The groundbreaking case was taken all the way to the Colorado Supreme Court and was one of the first lawsuits in the country that claimed damages for both physical and emotional distress. The brilliant legal work of his attorneys paid off, and Reese won a whopping $5,000 settlement in the case. While hobbling around on crutches, the Kid joked that the accident was his "lucky break." With the unexpected windfall, he bought a flashy new sports car despite his wife's objections. Unfortunately, waving at pretty girls got him into further trouble when he drove that new car into a ditch. The champ then wisely invested the rest of his compensation to placate his wife and bought a Colorado Avenue restaurant for them to operate.

Though teased by a few of his former comrades, David was all too happy to hang up his old boxing gloves and tie on his new apron strings. The retired pugilist soon mastered such local favorites as shepherd's pie, mutton stew and pan fried Rocky Mountain trout. His wife's cooking was also fabulous, and customers jokingly called her "Amazing Grace." The diner was conveniently located and open fourteen hours a day, and it became a home away from home for many. The hash-slinging duo known as Kid Montana and Amazing Grace often delighted diners by singing catchy tunes, and their impromptu performances earned them legions of loyal fans.

A few years later, the shadow of despair fell over the Reese household when David's former boxing mentor suddenly died at the restaurant's service counter. After he was taken to the undertakers, it was discovered that the fifty-five-year-old died from a ham sandwich, not from apoplexy, as first suspected. The coroner discovered the lump of fatty pork lodged in the man's throat after doing an autopsy. The sudden death of his good friend really knocked the former champ for a loop. David was often moody, and everyone joked that he needed to be handled with "Kid Gloves." The Kid lost interest not just in cooking but also in eating. In fact, the only thing the young husband and father seemed interested in doing was trying to satisfy his unquenchable thirst. Grace was left doing double duty on the homefront and at the diner, and she grew angry when her pleas for help fell on deaf ears. Arguments often escalated to knockdown, drag-out fights. The frustrated wife tried in vain to save face for the sake of their family but could no longer do so when newspapers screamed:

> *PRIZE FIGHTER CHALKS UP ANOTHER WIN!*
> *Mr. David Reese, also known as Kid Montana, the bonafide Prize fighter has scored again! Known from coast to coast for his impressive left jab, his opponent was floored in the first round as the Kid conquered in an unmatched victory! Mrs. Reese was left bruised, bloody, humiliated and disgraced before the spectators seated in the married couple's restaurant. Many of the diners were surprised to learn that dinner that evening*

Ghost orbs floating over the former Reese home. *Courtesy of Leon Waters.*

included a show and were disappointed when police closed the curtains on the performance by carting the pugilist away in the patty wagon and his defeated opponent, off in an ambulance.

While in custody at the El Paso County Jail, David Reese confessed to deputies that he was having violent thoughts and often dreamed of murdering his wife and children in their sleep. He feared that he would act on his impulse and begged to be kept in custody until his violent feelings subsided. He told detectives that he feared that he was going insane, and several tests were performed on him to assess his mental condition. However, after determining he was of sound mind, he was released from custody a few days later.

David was hopeful for a happy homecoming, but a "Dear John" letter, written by Grace, was taped to the front door. The note declared that she wanted a divorce and that she and the children would be living in the apartment above the restaurant. David began doing everything in his power to win back the love of his family. He quit drinking and even joined the First Baptist Church. However, Grace insisted that the marriage was over and made plans to move back to Kansas with their children.

The night before her farewell party, Grace was awakened from a deep sleep by a loud thud. When she turned on the lamp, she was bewildered to see her husband crawling through the apartment window. A lump lodged in her throat when she noticed the steel revolver clenched in his hand, but she managed to belt out a scream hoping to alert her children, who were sleeping in the next room. She begged for her life, but the drunken maniac argued that the only way to save their marriage was to kill the one who wanted out. The first bullet struck the bedside lamp, and glass shattered everywhere. The doomed woman screamed, much to the delight of the crazy fiend, and he laughed, seemingly amused by her fear. David fired another shot at his wife's head, but his lopsided aim missed its target and hit the bedroom floor instead. Undaunted by his poor marksmanship, the Kid fired a third and fourth shot. One bullet nicked a metal wire in Grace's corset, puncturing her lungs, and she withered to the floor like a deflated balloon. David was elated at the victory; he gathered her crumpled body in his arms, tenderly kissed her on the lips and then booted her out the second-story window.

Policeman R.F. Radar was patrolling the opposite side of the street and heard a volley of shots. He ran to the rescue and was aghast at the sight of the young woman splayed in a pool of blood on the sidewalk.

Noticing that she was miraculously still alive, he called for help and then climbed up a ladder left propped under a window in search of the screaming children. When Radar entered the dark apartment and turned on the light, he was horrified to discover Mr. David Reese sprawled on a blood-soaked bed with his shattered head lying next to him. Mrs. Reese miraculously regained consciousness at Bethel (Memorial) Hospital a short time later and recalled her husband's horrific assault. She whispered, "I know no reason why he should have wanted to kill me. I am sure he must have been out of his head at the time." No truer words have ever been spoken.

Doctors said that Grace might have survived the gunshot wound, but the fifteen-foot fall sealed her fate, and she sadly passed away hours later. A few days later, the *Colorado Springs Gazette* featured an article on August 19, 1921, headlined:

> *SEXTON'S SPADE HIDES LAST EVIDENCE OF DOUBLE TRAGEDY*
> *Two new graves dot the green in Fairview Cemetery. Three little orphans must today take up their fight for life alone—without parents or money, almost without friends.*
>
> *The graves hold the bodies of Grace Reese and David Reese. One was murdered and the other was a murderer.*

Shortly after the tragedy, the Reese children were placed on an orphan train bound for the West Coast. The restaurant closed and sat vacant for quite a while because many people believed the building was haunted. Finally, Fred's Bar moved into the building and was home to generations of barflies for many years. The little hole in the wall drew a wild bunch of cowboys, bikers and diehard drunks because it was the place you went to after you got kicked out of Roger's, which was just across the street. (Roger's is now called Dat's Italian.) Both bars were known to be haunted by spirits—and not just the kind you drink. Fred's became especially well known for its hauntings when a shadow of a man began appearing at the bar late at night. Old-timers remembered the sad tale of the drunken boxer who killed himself there long ago and began calling the lonely spirit the "Shadow Boxer." The ghost of Kid Montana became so popular that he even had his own stool at the end of the bar with his name painted on it.

For the past twenty years, a fine southwestern jewelry store known as the Flute Player has occupied the space where the infamous bar once stood. Some folks still claim to see the apparition of a dark shadow appearing in the windows above the store at 2511 Colorado late at night and believe it to be the ghostly Shadow Boxer. Perhaps Kid Montana does not realize that the fight has been over since 1921 and it's time for him to leave the ring.

For more information on the history of Old Colorado City, please visit the Old Colorado City History Center at 1 South Twenty-fourth Street in Colorado Springs or visit its website at history.oldcolo.com.

CITIES OF THE DEAD

EVERGREEN AND FAIRVIEW

Remember friends as you pass by
As you are now, so once was I
As I am now, so you must be
Prepare for death and follow me.
—*Epitaph in Evergreen Cemetery*

Every cemetery should have a ghost story, and historic Evergreen Cemetery has several. The fortress for the dead has been called a city within a city, and its archaic memorials represent a confluence of different cultures, races, ideas and religions. Evergreen was given to Colorado Springs by railroad pioneer and founding father General Palmer. The historic property stretches over two hundred acres of scenic rolling hills. Cows, goats, sheep and other farmyard critters grazed freely between the tombstones until fences were added. Eventually, the land was irrigated and cultivated, and rock gardens, benches and historic markers were added. In the 1950s, *Ripley's* called Evergreen the largest rose garden in the world; even today, citizens are proud of the city-owned cemetery, and it is often considered to be the crown jewel of Colorado Springs.

The old headstones of the cemetery are like an open history book. There are rags-to-riches stories, like that of carpenter turned mining mega millionaire Winfield Scott Stratton. The handsome bachelor was one of the city's greatest philanthropists; he died believing that his immense fortune caused him great despair. Then there are rags-to-riches-to-rags-again stories, like that of Robert Miller Womack. The miner's claim to fame happened when he got lucky in a cow pasture known as Poverty Gulch. The site of the gold strike later became known as the mining town of Cripple Creek, and the Pikes Peak or Bust gold rush began. Sadly, while in a drunken stupor, "Crazy Bob" traded his multimillion-dollar claim for some whiskey and quick cash. Later, he became an invalid and died in the poorhouse without a pot to pee in.

There are several impressive family mausoleums in Evergreen. The largest was built for the Giddings-Lennox families. Both clans became wealthy during the mining boom and had more money than they knew what to do with. So in 1903, they commissioned an architect and team of master craftsmen to construct a mausoleum that looks amazingly like a miniature version of the Parthenon—only better. Their shrine was furnished with stained-glass windows, something the Greeks never thought of. The cost to immortalize their names forever was a whopping $70,000, which would be about $1 million in 2012 dollars.

One family crypt still shrouded in mystery belongs to the former Mayor Bacon of Colorado Springs. Engineers constructed the mausoleum with thick fortress-like walls, and each casket was sealed inside a cement crypt that was locked shut. However, the tomb was still breached, and investigators are still baffled about how the thieves got inside. The cemetery manager called police after noticing vandalism outside the mausoleum. Together, they unlocked the ancient tomb and were shocked to discover that Mrs. Bacon's crypt had been pried open. The bone-chilling mystery only deepened when the wealthy woman's corpse was discovered to still be wearing an expensive pearl necklace. Investigators were further mystified when they found that the only thing missing from her coffin was her skull.

Mayor Bacon's family crypt in Evergreen Cemetery. *Courtesy of Blue Moon Haunted History Tours.*

48

The mausoleum was robbed almost twenty years ago, and yet the case is still unsolved today. It is unknown why the Bacon Mausoleum was targeted; if all the grave robbers wanted was a gruesome trophy, why didn't they dig up one of the thousands of graves in the paupers' field? Ever since the Bacon family tomb was raided, it has been rumored to be haunted and will likely remain so until Mrs. Bacon gets her head back where it belongs. It has been said that Mrs. Bacon's ghost glides through the cemetery on full moon nights dressed in a long black evening gown. A pearl necklace dangles precariously from the shoulders of her headless skeleton. Local ghost hunters believe that the mayor's wife is still searching for the thieves who desecrated her family's tomb and her ghost stalks the cemetery like a lioness at night.

Cemetery volunteer Mike Coletta has seen a lot of strange things while leading tour groups through local graveyards, but none can top what he saw one night while leading a tour group through Evergreen. Out of the corner of his eye, he saw what could only be described as a panther-like creature. It was black and about five feet long and flew through the air without making a sound. He turned to a startled tour participant and asked if the man had seen anything strange, and the guy confirmed that he had. So Mike asked him to write down exactly what he saw, and Mike did the same. Then the two men compared notes before the group and realized that they had both described the same creature. Mike is not sure what he saw that night, but he knows that it was not of this world. Could it have been the ghost of Mrs. Bacon?

The little stone chapel inside Evergreen Cemetery is on the National Register of Historic Places. Funeral services were held there for generations, and the basement was used as cold storage for up to three dozen dead bodies at a time. The morgue under the church was a morbid necessity because during the winter the earth was too frozen for the undertaker's spade. Naked corpses were laid out to dry on concrete slabs, and heavy iron bloating balls were placed on top to crush gas out of the bodies as they decayed. Body fluid stains can still be seen on the cement beds and floor and serve as a gruesome visual reminder of the chapel's creepy history.

In September 2010, cemetery volunteer Coletta was doing a paranormal investigation in the basement morgue when he caught evidence of a ghost on camera. While using a K2 meter, the device started registering high electromagnetic frequencies. Mike responded and turned on a video camera just as a heavy crypt door slowly pushed open of its own accord. He placed the astonishing evidence on YouTube and was surprised when producers from the Biography Channel saw the video and contacted him. Coletta and city cemetery manager William De Boer flew to California to film for a program called *My Ghost Story*. The feature was shown in April 2011 and can still be seen on YouTube.

With so many dead people lying around, it would be difficult to guess who haunts the chapel. However, ghost hunters have concluded that the ghost is a suicide victim named Delos Powell. Powell was the first sexton of Evergreen Cemetery. He was also a city alderman and belonged to a couple fraternal organizations. By all accounts, Delos Powell was a hardworking, upstanding citizen who was highly regarded in society. That's why it was shocking to the community when the newspaper announced that the sexton was skimming money from the cemetery books and bribing other city leaders to bury his dirty secret. After being released on bond, Powell drove to Evergreen Cemetery with murder in his heart. Moments later the desperate man was found lying in a pool of blood with a bullet hole in his head AND a drained bottle of rat poison clutched in his hand. Oddly, he was still alive, and a hearse driver rushed him to Bethel (Memorial) Hospital, where three doctors were called to try and save his life. But it was too late, and he died on the operating table. One attending physician wryly noted that Powell's ambitious suicide technique was just a bit "overkill."

The *Colorado Springs Gazette Telegraph* noted the somber funeral of the city alderman on June 25, 1904, with a headline that stated the brutal facts: "Friends of Delos Powell View Remains before Funeral Burial of Late City Sexton. Will Be in Cemetery that Proved His Undoing. Services Will Be Private."

Immediately after Powell was laid to rest, dozens of people applied for his good-paying job. Strange as it may sound, every new hire either quit or died within a year. Many people believed it was because the ghost of Delos Powell didn't want anyone else taking his prestigious job. His ghost was seen for years afterward, still wearing his trademark wide-brimmed hat. Sometimes he was seen by the front gates and, in later years, inside the chapel. Many folks still see him around today, even one hundred years after his death.

Fairview Cemetery could be considered the country cousin of the crosstown elegant Evergreen and is documented as being extremely haunted. Several gunslingers, outlaws and even a runaway slave are buried in its keep, as well as a few soiled doves from the notorious red-light district. Laura Bell McDaniel was one of the most successful madams in the history of the Old West. She was well known for catering to the upper class, her

Here Lies
Steve and Anya

In eternal bliss
Mastercard & Visa still
looking for the payments
they missed

Schuetze   Wittenberg
July 11, 1961   Sept. 25, 1944
Mar. 29, 2009

An amusing headstone seen in
Fairview Cemetery. *Courtesy of Full
Moon Explorations.*

strong business sense and her unusual way of advertising. The cunning madam and her good friend Prairie Dog O'Byrne used to hitch a pair of tame elk named Thunder and Buttons to a decorated wagon and parade their well-dressed ladies around town. The advertising gimmick worked; McDaniel was soon one of the most successful madams in the red-light district.

Being queen of the tenderloin afforded her the best lot in Fairview Cemetery. Unfortunately, not long after purchasing the premium plot, she died in a mysterious car accident. It was well known that law enforcement wanted to run the loose ladies from town, and many folks believed that someone tampered with the brakes on Laura Bell's brand-new luxury car. Despite the suspicion over her untimely death, Laura Bell seemed to be resting in peace at Fairview—until her family uprooted her grave to a new location. Not long after the invasion, Laura Bell was seen dressed in all her finery scowling at visitors as she leaned against her massive headstone. Many folks believe she still haunts the graveyard to this day because she is not happy lying next to the cemetery restrooms.

Blanche Burton, another famous Colorado City madam, is buried near Laura Bell and was also killed under mysterious circumstances. On December 20, 1909, Chief McDowell and Patrolman Morse heard screaming and turned to see a woman running down Colorado Avenue with her nightgown on fire. An unidentified man was also seen running from the scene. Many people believe that the stranger threw an oil lamp at the prostitute and sent her running out the door on fire. The hot-to-trot victim was later identified as infamous madam Blanche Burton. Sadly, just the day before her mysterious death, the "hooker with a heart of gold" gave away her last bucket of coal to a family in need. Blanche was financially destitute and would have been buried in the paupers' cemetery if it had not been for the kindness of fellow madam Mamie Rogers. Miss Rogers paid for the gloomy funeral service, which was held on a snowy Christmas Eve. The dismal ghost of Blanche was often seen after her death, crying near her unmarked grave until concerned city leaders decided to buy her a proper headstone in 1983. The simple marker reads:

Pioneer Madam
Blanche Burton
1859–1909
The Sins of the Living
Are not of the Dead

Miraculously, after placing the simple heart-shaped headstone, the haunting ceased, and Blanche now appears to be at rest.

The most infamous ghost to haunt the spooky cemetery is Zadia Morrison Ryan. Ghost hunters warn not to speak her married name within earshot of her grave because they fear that doing so will bring on her horrible vengeance. Her angry spirit has been causing problems in the graveyard for over a century, and her rage grows even fiercer as time goes by. Zadia's sad story began over one hundred years ago when she met an innocent country boy who would literally throw her life down the crapper.

Earl Ryan was just a kid when he moved with his folks from Missouri to Colorado City. The boy told Zadia he loved her the first day they met and even asked for her hand in marriage. Their engagement lasted three long years until they were old enough to wed; Earl was eighteen, and his child bride was just fifteen. The newlyweds were as happy as two peas in a pod living in a little cottage on Lincoln Street. Unfortunately, paradise was lost after Earl was fired from his job and took to the bottle in despair. After wallowing in sorrow for a good long time, Earl ventured to Fort Garland and was hired by the local teamsters. The romantic Romeo sent loving letters filled with sweet nothings home to his child bride. One of these heartfelt letters was later published in the *Colorado Springs Gazette Telegraph* in February 1908 and reads:

Dear Wife,
I will send $10.00 the tenth of February; that will be enough for you to come to me…I would have sent money a long time ago but you know the way you done once with the money…now it is almost supper time and I will write you again after I eat, but I don't know how good it will be… Supper is over and will finish your dear letter…If you don't come when I send you the money I don't know what to do…Goodnight dear. From Earl, to dear wife Zadia. Please don't forget me.

Evidence of the destructive wrath of Zadia Ryan in Fairview Cemetery. *Courtesy of Colorado Ghost Tours LLC.*

Earl dutifully sent money to Zadia as promised and waited patiently for her reply. But days went by without a hoot or holler from his dearly beloved wife. Lonely and depressed, Earl went to the local bar and spilled his heart out to a stranger. The bartender listened to his saga and then said he coincidently knew a pretty gal named Zadia, but her last name was Morrison, not Ryan. Then he added that he'd had a date with her in Colorado City just the week before and quipped that she was by far the cutest little tart in the entire red-light district. After hitting the guy over the head with a beer bottle, Earl packed his bags and hopped the midnight train to Colorado City. He was thirsty as hell when he got there, so to wet his whistle he bought a pint of whiskey and drained it before reaching home.

Earl didn't recognize the beautiful, blurry woman who opened the door of his home. However, it soon dawned on him that the little girl he had left behind a year earlier was now a full-grown woman. His wife's long dark braids were pinned in a bun, and she was perfumed, powdered and rouged. He grew weak in the knees at the sight of her cherubic face and tried to break the ice by using keen wit and charm. Thinking quickly, he removed his hat, politely introduced himself and then offered a shiny new nickel for a date. Zadia was not amused by his sarcasm and added injury to his insult by hitting him over the head with a frying pan. A terrific fight ensued; first a satin slipper was thrown, then a picture frame and then a lamp. When all the furniture in the house was busted, they took their brawl to the street. The screaming and shouting seemed to go on forever, and neighbors were greatly relieved when the fireworks ended about midnight.

Little more was thought of Earl's volatile homecoming until a few days later when Zadia's mother went calling. When she heard that Earl was back in town, she became greatly alarmed and engaged friends to join in the search. A few hours later, a neighbor found Earl lying dead in the alley outhouse. Coroner Law did a thorough investigation of the latrine and sadly discovered Zadia's corpse there as well. He theorized that the jealous man had killed his wife and then attempted to hide the murder by stuffing her body down the poop shoot. Earl must have realized the plan was fudged when methane gas pushed Zadia's broken body to the surface. The young man must have become frustrated by his futile attempts and apparently ended the debacle in suicide. Although prostrate with grief, Mrs. Morrison blamed the tragedy entirely on Zadia's wild ways and claimed that she had done everything in her power to persuade her to join her husband in Fort Garland. According to attorney W.D. Lombard, Zadia was saving money to file for divorce, claiming cruelty and desertion. In an ironic twist of fate, the couple's funeral was held on their two-year anniversary. On February 10, 1908, the sad headlines of the *Colorado Springs Gazette Telegraph* read:

> *DOUBLE FUNERAL HELD*
> *VICTIMS OF DOUBLE TRAGEDY LAID TO REST*
> *SEVERAL HUNDRED PEOPLE ATTEND CEREMONY*
> *MAN'S PARENTS' ALMOST PROSTRATED*
> *Side by side in the same grave, in Fairview cemetery, Colorado City, the bodies of Earl Ryan and his wife Zadia, were laid to rest yesterday. At 2:30 o'clock, the chapel at Minimum's undertaking rooms…several hundred curious people thronged the street waiting for a chance to view the remains.*

It was not long after the funeral that Zadia started haunting Fairview Cemetery. Legend tells that the mournful woman is not at peace because she shares an underground tomb with the man who murdered her long ago. Many people claim to hear a scratching noise when they walk by the headstone of the doomed lovers and believe Zadia's ghost is trying to dig her way out of the dirt prison. Zadia's luminous presence is also seen by her grave wearing a long red gown, and she often carries dead flowers in a wicker basket. Her angry spirit has been haunting Fairview Cemetery for over one hundred years, and the havoc that she causes there is troublesome. What is even more startling to cemetery staff is that her vindictive spirit seems only to grow angrier as the years go by. On the one-hundred-year anniversary of Zadia's death, several ancient fifty-foot-tall evergreen trees near her grave were ripped from the ground by their roots. All five of the trees were healthy, leaving cemetery workers at a loss for words when asked to explain the mystery. However, legions of Zadia's believers know why it happened and even who was responsible for the mayhem. They explain that until her grave is exhumed and she is reburied away from her murdering husband, her horrific paranormal temper tantrums will only intensify as the years go by.

GRAY GHOSTS OF THE OLD RAILROAD DEPOT

But there is a fatality, a feeling so irresistible and inevitable that it has the force of doom, which almost invariably compels human beings to linger around and haunt, ghost-like, the spot where some great and marked event has given the color to their lifetime; and still the more irresistibly, the darker the tinge that saddens it.
—*Nathaniel Hawthorne,* The Scarlet Letter

Legends and ghost stories about haunted trains have been popular for as long as there has been an iron horse, and these spooky tales about the rails have became a big part of American folklore. Colorado Springs, like many other cities, would not even be on the map were it not for the help of the railroad. Founding father General Palmer was a pioneer in the railroad industry, and it was because of his influence that the Denver and Rio Grand Railroad (D&RG) came to town in 1871. Although considered to be a safe mode of transportation, deadly collisions and derailments were inevitable. Accidents were so common that some train depots had a morgue room called a "Dead House" to store bodies of the deceased until the coroner was notified. Railroad engineers as a class were known to be a superstitious lot, and spinning yarns was a good way to pass the time. Not long after the rails were laid, spooky legends, ghost stories and other strange tales began to spread from coast to coast. The ghost story about the beautiful suicidal woman lying naked across the tracks has been known for well over one hundred years. No one knows if the legend is true, but it certainly helped to keep a few overworked engineers awake at night.

Legends of ghost trains have also been popular in American folklore. The most well-known tale is of President Lincoln's haunted funeral train. After the president was assassinated in 1865, his body was transported from Washington, D.C., back to his home in Springfield, Illinois. The somber cortege was draped in black tulle and passed slowly down the tracks. People lined up for miles along the route to pay their last respects to the fallen hero. Legend says that as Lincoln's funeral train passed through each town, clocks and watches mysteriously stopped ticking. Over 140 years later, the strange phenomenon still occurs on the anniversary of Lincoln's death. The iron horse is shrouded in black, and mourning flags flap silently without wind. The mysterious image glows in the moonlight and glides silently down the tracks; it has been seen by many awestruck witnesses. In 1937, residents in the Hudson Valley claimed to have seen menacing skeletons waving from the windows of Lincoln's ghost train. That same year in Iowa, Robert Hefflon became so spooked by the phantom image that he threw rocks at it and was promptly arrested. Throwing rocks at ghost trains is not illegal in Iowa, but stoning people who walk in front of ghost trains *is*, and Robert Hefflon was charged with assault because a passing stranger was injured in the incident.

It is not just lunatics who have seen the frightening apparition. The *Albany Times* wrote:

> *After the pilot engine passes, the funeral train itself with flags and streamers rushes past. The track seems covered with black carpet and the coffin is seen in the center of the car, while all about it in the air and on the train behind are vast numbers of blue coated men, some with coffins on their backs, others leaning onto them.*

Another popular railroad ghost legend concerns gray ladies. These ghosts are said to be the spirits of women who died waiting for their lovers to return from afar. The color gray refers to their emotional state, and they always have mournful expressions on their faces. One well-known local railroad legend is of a gray lady who was seen on the old D&RG line. The ghost story claims that a Palmer Lake schoolteacher became secretly engaged to a man who worked for the railroad. One night, she packed up her things and waited for him at the gazebo near the tracks. The young lovers were planning to elope together, but when her betrothed did not show as planned, the scorned woman committed suicide. Legend says that shortly after the incident, her gray ghost was seen standing in the gazebo; other times, it has been spotted along the tracks between Colorado Springs and Palmer Lake.

Engineers on the Midland line that ran from Colorado Springs over the great divide also saw her tragic ghost, and she made national headlines when the *Charlotte Observer* reported her story on November 18, 1901:

> *TRAINMEN BOTHERED BY SPOOKS*
> *Engineer Gene Smith of Colorado Midland doesn't believe in ghosts and that's what troubles him. He was rounding a deep hull near King station, one day this week when he saw the figure of a woman dressed in grey lying across the track. "It was too late to apply the brakes," he said to a group of trainmen today. "I gave the whistle. It was an echo of the despairing wail that rose from my heart. I closed my eyes but we struck nothing. Looking out from the engine a moment later I saw before me floating up and with the hand waving mockingly at me the figure for which I had just seen lying prostrate on the tracks." J.D. Cowley, who runs another train over the same route, confirms Smith's story. Both are men of unquestionable voracity. There is much apprehension over train men on that branch and it is said that there is a strong demand for rabbits' feet and other talismans.*

Gray ghosts can also be spirits of mournful men who died waiting for their lovers. There is a very famous story of one such spirit that haunts the D&RG depot in Colorado Springs. He is believed to be the ghost of George Obendorfer, a German immigrant from Cincinnati who died while vacationing in Colorado Springs. The tourist's sad story began long ago when he became the last victim of the infamous cold-blooded serial killer known as "Arsenic Annie." The story begins when Arsenic Annie was known as Anna Matscheki. The beautiful young woman was a medical student and wife to Dr. Matscheki in Vienna. After becoming pregnant, she dropped her studies and gave birth to their son, Oscar. The couple was happy until the affluent doctor died suddenly of a mysterious illness. Grief-stricken, Anna buried her husband and sailed over the pond to begin life anew with an aunt and uncle in Cincinnati's German-flavored Over-the-Rhine district. The charming widow spoke both English and German fluently and soon made many friends; however, she spent most of her time with a much older widower named Phillip Hahn. Soon, the unlikely duo fell in love, and they were married within the year.

A few months later, Anna's aunt and uncle suddenly died, and she used her inheritance to purchase a little German delicatessen. The busy restaurant did so well that within two years the Hahns opened a second location. However, pushing sauerkraut, sausage and wieners was not the glamorous life in America that the pretty blond immigrant had imagined. So for cheap thrills, she began sneaking off to the horse track in Kentucky, and what started out as innocent fun soon landed her deep in debt. Desperate for money, Anna next gambled on insurance fraud. After three suspicious fires, Mr. Hahn discovered his wife's secret addiction to gambling and fraud and said he would rat her out if she didn't clean up her act. The flaxen-haired vixen responded by trying to poison him—not just once but twice! Mr. Hahn was flabbergasted when he discovered that the merry widow had taken out two large life insurance policies on him before the assault, and he moved out of their home just as fast as he could pack a bag.

Anna didn't grieve the loss for long and soon set her sights on other studs in the corral. While doing volunteer nursing work, she met retired rancher Jacob Wagner, and his comrades were completely stupefied when he pronounced his love for the Bavarian bombshell. The smitten rancher threw a lavish surprise engagement party for his future bride. However, the elaborate white-tie shindig ended on a sour note after a neighbor regurgitated all over the buffet table. The retired schoolteacher spent two days in the hospital, and doctors were perplexed about what had caused the sudden illness. To make matters worse, the old woman's apartment was robbed while she was incapacitated, but this went unnoticed for days because Jacob Wagner's death got all the attention. Sadly, the affable rancher was found dead the morning after the party, and everyone in the apartment building was traumatized by his untimely demise.

Anna became adept at luring lonely old men away from their fortunes by filling their empty hearts and stomachs. The seductress might have gotten her secret recipes from the Lucrezia Borgia cookbook, *Poisoning for Dummies*; however, she discovered many deadly secrets on her own. The former medical student learned the art of concealing the acidic taste of arsenic by sprinkling the poison over food. Another slick trick of the merry widow involved croton oil, which she used to cleanse the chemical residue from the colon. The common home remedy was odorless, tasteless, cheap and easily found in most drugstores. (Side effects were troublesome, however, as sudden explosive bouts of diarrhea were common.) Anna seemed to enjoy her challenging new occupation in nursing. She often quipped that although the work was demanding, the pay was good, and she liked making her own hours. Once patients were penniless, she would begin tampering with their food. Sometimes she would intermittently poison her victims by allowing them to linger a while in her deceitful web like a spider toying with a trapped fly. In just eight years' time, it was estimated that the wicked widow murdered over a dozen men. The femme fatale's modus operandi was consistent, and Anna might have gotten away with killing dozens more if not for her last victim—George Obendorfer.

George Obendorfer was a retired German cobbler who told friends that it was love at first sight when he met his so-called German strudel in a local bakery. The love-struck Valentino even shaved off his thick gray mustache and started wearing dentures to look younger for his sweetheart. The happy couple soon made plans to take eight-year-old Oscar on a train trip during summer vacation so he could see some real cowboys and Indians in Colorado. Just before heading out of town, George told neighbors that he was thinking about riding off into the sunset with his dream gal and joked that he might never return.

On the evening of July 30, the trio arrived at the D&RG depot in Colorado Springs. Anna and Oscar checked into the affluent Antlers Hotel while George stumbled across the park looking for a cheaper place to stay. He got a room at the Park Hotel on the corner of Tejon and Pikes Peak (now a bank) but was too sick to retrieve his luggage from the depot lockers. Anna and Oscar didn't let the sick old man ruin their vacation; the next morning, they were up at dawn to ride the cog railroad up Pikes Peak. When they

An antique postcard of the second Antlers Hotel. *Author's collection.*

reached the summit, they playfully tossed snowballs and gleefully posed for scrapbook photos. That afternoon, they toured the Cave of the Winds in Manitou Springs and had lunch in Monument Valley Park. Two days later, the blond Borgia and Oscar hightailed it to the mile-high city, where Anna sold two diamond rings at a Denver pawnshop. Then they continued their journey back to Cincinnati—without George Obendorfer.

On August 1, 1937, Memorial Hospital contacted the Colorado Springs police about an attractive blond woman who had abandoned an indigent old man in the emergency room. Staff told police that the poor old German so despaired at being left there that he grabbed his coat and wobbled out of the hospital calling, "Strudel, Strudel! *Ich liebe dich!*" Sadly, a few hours later, the desperate stranger was found dead. After interviewing German-speaking witnesses at the train depot, they learned that the old man was staying at the Park Hotel. Investigators found the information intriguing because the owner of the Park Hotel had just filed a theft report about two missing diamond rings. Inside a train station locker, they found George Obendorfer's suitcase packed with clothes, a pipe, some tobacco and a silver saltshaker containing 82 percent arsenic dioxide. A funeral notice was posted for George Obendorfer in the *Colorado Springs Gazette Telegraph* on August 2, 1937:

> *Private funeral services for George Obendorfer, 67-year-old Cincinnati cobbler died here August the first under mysterious circumstances, were held yesterday at the law funeral home's drawing room, the Rev. W.G. Schaefer, pastor of the United Brethren church, officiating. Burial was in Evergreen cemetery here.*

Cincinnati police arrested Anna Hahn on charges of grand larceny of two diamond rings from the Park Hotel; however, what they were really interested in was why she left a dead old man behind. After doing a thorough investigation, police suspected that the so-called nurse had murdered several other senior citizens as well. Despite the fact that most of the evidence was circumstantial, prosecutors brought the case to trial, charging Mrs. Anna Marie Hahn for murdering Jacob Wagner and two other elderly Germans who had died mysteriously under her care. Amazingly, the she-devil maintained her innocence throughout the trial even though a handwriting expert proved her deception. When Anna took the witness stand, she confidently explained that she used poison for exterminating pests, not people, and the croton oil was for her frequent constipation. However, the prosecution snidely retorted that she possessed enough poison in her home to kill half of Cincinnati. The next day, newspapers across the country dubbed her "Arsenic Annie," and the media circus began. Thousands of curiosity-seekers from all over the country arrived at the courthouse daily in hopes of getting a glimpse of the infamous femme fatale.

The first witness was George Weis, who swore under oath that Anna Marie Hahn had sprinkled poison in his beer and that he permanently lost the use of his legs as a result. Dozens of other witnesses testified against her character, including Oscar and even her estranged husband. To add dramatic appeal, forensic evidence was gruesomely displayed in the courtroom, including the arsenic-riddled organs of her victims.

A month later, Anna sat motionless when the guilty verdict was announced. Public defenders kept the court system busy with appeals that were taken all the way to the Ohio Supreme Court. However, her date in the hot seat was imminent, and when a last-chance midnight call from the governor didn't happen, she began her solemn walk to the death chamber. Arsenic Annie passed out on the floor when she saw the electric chair, and officials had to revive her with an ammonia vial before strapping her into the killing machine. Then the chaplain recited the Lord's Prayer, and the hooded executioner pulled the switch. Arsenic Annie looked like a crazed marionette as the electric wires delivered the raging punch to her brain. The pretty blond thirty-one-year-old was pronounced dead at 12:05 a.m. on December 7, 1938.

Meanwhile, 75 years later, the gray ghost of old George still haunts the D&RG depot in downtown Colorado Springs. Some people believe he loiters around the depot because a trial was never held for his murder. Other folks think maybe he is still waiting for his beloved strudel to take him home to Cincinnati. If that is the case, he will be haunting the joint for a long time because the last passenger train left the station in 1971. In 1973, the old depot on Sierra Madre Street was saved from the wrecking ball and became known as Giuseppe's Depot Italian Restaurant. The depot still looks much like it did 125 years ago. Inside the lobby, you will find twenty-five-foot-tall pine ceilings and original floor tiles dating to 1887. The restaurant houses a treasure-trove of antiques, and many photographs from the railroad's golden era grace the walls. Employees don't mind working with a ghost and even joke that it can be fun. Anytime something goes missing, they have a ready-made scapegoat in George. They blame the ghost for everything from flushing all the toilets in unison to shutting off the lights in the Pullmans Lounge on command.

An antique postcard of the D&RG depot. *Author's collection.*

Adrianna Carvalho worked at the restaurant for several years while attending Colorado College. She said that the old depot is especially haunted by the hostess station, where it is believed George's dead body was found. The front of the building is where the storage lockers used to be, and that is where the ghost of old George is still seen, apparently searching for his suitcase. His eerie gray transparent figure has also been seen pacing back and forth down the railroad track. Many people think George Obendorfer is seen at the train station as a gray ghost because the woman he loved poisoned and abandoned him in an unfamiliar town, leaving him a stranger in a strange land. Will old George haunt the depot forever? Ghost hunters think he will, at least until he finally realizes that he is not in the land of the living. Either way, it's the end of the line for old George.

DOWNTOWN SPIRITS OF
JUSTICE AND JINX

Heaven has no rage like love to hatred turned,
Nor hell a fury like a woman scorned.
—*William Congreve,* The Mourning Bride

Museums, especially old ones, always seem to be haunted, and the Pioneer Museum in downtown Colorado Springs is no exception. The massive concrete block-and-granite fortress is a treasure-trove of history that started with collections donated by the Pioneer Association in 1907. Some of the first items to be displayed were the dueling pistol carried by the first town marshal, the hatchet used in a century-old murder mystery and a whiskey bottle that once touched the lips of George Washington. The collection has grown to be quite impressive over the last hundred years and now includes several awards for excellence, making the Pioneer Museum the glory of Colorado Springs and all of Colorado as well.

The Pioneer Museum was originally built as the El Paso County Courthouse in 1903. The grand structure was designed in a Second Renaissance revival style and was the inspiration of local architect August J. Smith. The three-story building is surrounded by a park, and it sits on a pedestal of stairs. The most astonishing feature is the clock tower, which looms over downtown Colorado Springs like a colossal eye in the sky. Thankfully, the museum is now protected as a historic landmark; just a few decades ago, the glorious building with ornate wrought iron, marbled pillars and pink granite floors was a target for the wrecking ball.

An antique postcard of the haunted Pioneer Museum. *Author's collection.*

If the courtroom walls could talk, they might tell amusing stories about shotgun weddings or the murder trial where the disgruntled housewife killed her drunken husband with a rolling pin at the Sleepy Valley trailer village. They might also tell about a horrific killing that happened within its keep. The brutal murder in the El Paso County Courthouse made national headlines, and the ghost that remained after the deadly assault has been recognized ever since. The haunting story begins with Eddie Beals, whose friends called him the "Small Wonder" because of his short stature and athletic prowess. After graduating from Cheyenne Mountain High School, Beals started a business conducting hiking tours up Pikes Peak and was quite successful. When he was in his early thirties, he got a job with the county, and after twenty years he had worked his way up to chief custodian. He was very proud to have his own office at the El Paso County Courthouse, even if it was just a broom closet with a desk. After his big promotion, it was obvious that the little man suffered from the dreadful Napoleon complex. When employees heard his keys jingling down the hallway, they scattered like flies knowing that "Mr. Clean" was making white glove spot checks. Many heads rolled under Mr. Beals's nitpicky regime, and employees feared the ruthless administrator.

In 1959, tension in the workplace mounted when Mr. Beals began having personal problems. After twenty years of marriage, his wife wanted a divorce. She claimed that Eddie was always at work so he may as well live there. Mr. Beals agreed; he packed his things and moved into the caretaker's apartment above the courthouse. The pint-sized tyrant even manipulated staff to help him move over the weekend without pay. A janitor named Willie Butler accidently ripped a cheap throw rug, and Mr. Beals squawked, "Watch whatcha doin' ya big dummy!" Mr. Beals even had the nerve to dock Butler's pay eleven dollars to buy a new rug. When the short-stacked administrator moved into his bachelor's pad, he began to enjoy the swinging single life and all that it entailed. The first thing he did was trade in his beat-up jalopy for a Corvette and his old coveralls for cheap polyester suits. The Small Wonder proudly flaunted his new lifestyle and strutted around the courthouse like a cock in a henhouse, acting like God's gift to women. One day, Willie Butler caught his boss making goo-goo eyes at his wife, and the jealous janitor almost belted the pipsqueak in the kisser.

A few weeks later, Willie Butler was looking forward to Memorial Day weekend and went to pick up his paycheck, which was already two days late. When it wasn't at the main office, he decided to go directly to Mr. Beals, even though it was against proper protocol. Willie almost laughed when he read the handmade sign, "Private! Eddie Beals, Chief Custodian," taped to the closet door. When his boss opened the door, red lipstick was smeared on his upper lip, making him look like a kid with a Kool-Aid mustache. Before Willie had a chance to apologize for the intrusion, the little ladies' man squeaked, "Whatcha want ya big dummy?" Several administrators standing in the hallway snickered when they overheard the snide remark. Without saying a word, the humiliated janitor snatched his paycheck off the desk but accidently knocked a cup of pencils onto the floor. Beals squawked at him again and then kicked Willie in the butt for good measure.

As Willie drove home, he thought about his pigheaded boss, and it made his blood boil. To cool off, he stopped at Murphy's Bar, and with one gulp Butler ended a seven-year itch. Willie had been sober since moving from the small town of Gonzales, Texas. The fifty-five-year-old janitor had a hard life in the Longhorn State. After dropping out of high school, he had married his pregnant girlfriend and soon became a chicken farmer with a drinking problem. The couple had eight children who ranged in age from five to twenty-five, and his eldest daughter, a court stenographer, had helped him get the coveted government job.

After a liquid lunch, Willie ran some errands and then drove to the courthouse to begin the night shift. When he walked into the basement employee lounge, he could hear Eddie screaming down the hall and that old familiar feeling of dread and despair punched him in the gut. That's when he reached in his coat pocket for a cigarette and instead felt the salvation of a .38-caliber revolver. Suddenly he recalled getting his gun out of the pawnshop just hours earlier and the thought of killing the little weasel filled his heart with joy. While giddily loading the bullets into the gun's chamber, Willie Butler reasoned that he would be doing everyone at work a favor by rubbing out the Small Wonder.

Murder should never be committed on an empty stomach, so Willie stopped and ate a hot dog in the cafeteria. He then calmly went upstairs and hid behind Mr. Beals's office door. When the despotic ruler returned to his throne room, the drunken janitor flipped on the lights and pounced on his prey. However, the Small Wonder took the brawny brute to the mat and pummeled his chest with both fists. Seconds later, Willie overthrew his opponent, but still not satisfied with the victory, he grabbed a cup of Ticonderoga #2 pencils and snapped every one of them, tossing the broken pieces into the air like confetti. Eddie Beals stood quivering like a cornered mouse, not knowing what to expect next as Willie went wild and declared war. Willie Butler threw grenades of sponges and scrub brushes; a box of powdered soap exploded like napalm. The jaded janitor complained about everything from working split shifts to the dried-out hot dogs in the cafeteria. For the grand finale, he pulled a pistol from his pocket and made his boss cry uncle before firing all six shots. As Eddie Beals lay dying on the floor, Willie Butler laughed maniacally and said, "I hope that will satisfy you." Then he walked triumphantly out of the office, still holding the smoking gun.

A courthouse secretary heard the gunshots and saw Willie Butler calmly walking out the west side doors. She joked, "Did you do that, Willie Butler?" Butler grinned from ear to ear and boasted, "I sure did." Then she chided him once more and said, "Oh no you didn't." He smiled again, saying, "Oh yes I did!" Then he triumphantly walked down the sidewalk like the weight of the world had lifted from his shoulders.

The sheriff soon caught up with him, and proud Willie surrendered without incident. When questioned by detectives, Butler calmly rolled cigarettes and talked of good southern cooking, bragging about his secret recipe for collard greens and chitlins. Investigators discovered that Willie Butler had murdered before—ten years earlier, at his chicken ranch in Texas. He confessed to killing in self-defense—the defense of his chickens!

He claimed that his neighbor's pigs kept knocking down the fence and killing his livestock. When the problem began to affect his livelihood, the drunkard loaded up his shotgun and served his neighbor some Texas justice. The judge ordered a five-year stint in the state penitentiary, but Willie Butler was released on parole in half that time.

There was a bit of tragic irony when Willie Butler took the witness stand just footsteps away from where he had murdered his boss. After the testimony of dozens of witnesses, it looked like curtains for the confessed two-time killer. However, the silver-tongued devil was a gifted showman and was able to convince the jury that his tyrannical boss drove him to drink and commit the desperate act. After just a half hour of deliberation, the jury handed down the verdict of involuntary manslaughter, and the judge sentenced the chicken farmer/janitor to eight years of hard labor. Willie Butler served just two years and then was paroled and moved to California. Eddie Beals, however, had never moved on. His ghost has been haunting the old courthouse ever since he was assassinated there over fifty years ago. Employees say that Eddie's ghost is very friendly because he often opens doors for visitors, rides along with guests in the old birdcage elevator and will respond to his name when called.

Several paranormal investigation groups have visited the old courthouse over the years and have unanimously confirmed the building to be haunted, not by just one ghost, but at least two. Another ghost of a woman wearing a gray dress and riding boots has been seen on the third floor of the museum. Chuck Newsome was head of security in 1999 when he saw the apparition of the lady in gray on several occasions. The grey ghost is believed to be the spirit of Laura Mathews, a well-known stage actress who died in Colorado Springs in 1908. Employees figure that Laura's ghost still haunts the courthouse because she was not happy with the verdict of her murder case.

Laura Mathews was born in Kansas City in 1888 and blossomed into a beautiful young woman with flowing locks of auburn hair and eyes of emerald green. The talented beauty left home for New York City when she was just sixteen years old in search of fame and fortune. She became one of the most sought-after actresses of her time, and she traveled all over the country for engagements and had fans in every city. No matter where she went, her dressing room brimmed with gifts from ardent fans. In the summer of 1906, she performed in a musical in Chicago and was astonished when a truckload of long-stemmed pink roses was delivered to her dressing room. The card attached simply requested a meeting with her; it was signed "C.C."

Laura was instantly attracted to the interesting and exciting Mr. Chas Coey when she met him. The silver fox claimed that he was an accomplished man by the time he was forty and next wanted to marry and start a family. Laura fell head over heels for the dashing millionaire, and the May-December romance flourished until a few months later, when a skeleton fell out of Coey's closet and the thud reverberated across Chicago. Mr. Coey had a dirty little secret: a blond fiancée named Victoria. Laura discovered the deception when his engagement to the debutante was announced in the society column. Victoria was from the right side of the tracks, and Laura was not. The award-winning actress put on the performance of a lifetime when she confronted Coey about his deceit. She fell on his doorstep, kicking, screaming and pleading for him to break off the engagement. When that failed, she left in a huff saying that she would rather die than ever see his face again. The next day, Laura fled by train to Colorado Springs and checked into the Acacia Hotel with eighteen trunks and her nursemaid, Miss Tillie Green. The new grand hotel had just opened its doors for business a few weeks earlier, and Laura was delighted when she got a spacious corner suite with a view of Pikes Peak.

The next day, Laura ventured across the street to Acacia Park for a lawn concert. It was quite a surprise when she bumped into an acquaintance

An antique postcard of the Acacia Hotel. *Author's collection.*

from Chicago, a wealthy businessman by the name of Amos Rumbaugh. Mr. Rumbaugh was coincidently an associate of Mr. Coey and told her he was staying just a block away at the Alta Vista Hotel. After the concert was over, he offered to escort her back to her hotel. As they walked, she confided that Mr. Coey was a playboy who had strung her along with sweet promises. Rumbaugh listened to the teenager like a father; he offered a shoulder for her to cry on and then kindly dried her tears. Laura was enjoying the comforting conversation until Rumbaugh suddenly admitted his true love for her. When the actress got back to her room, she told Tillie about the strange encounter with Rumbaugh and complained that he reeked of whiskey.

The next morning, Tillie went to Laura's room and was frantic to find she was gone. The bellhop said that the actress had gone for a late-night horseback ride but never returned. Tillie went to the Alta Vista Hotel and told Rumbaugh of the situation, imploring him to help her search for Laura. Meanwhile, in the nearby town of Ivywild, a saddled horse was seen wandering a meadow without a rider. A farmer went to investigate and found a beautiful young woman dead on a dirt road with an ivory-handled Remington pistol clutched in one hand and a tear-stained suicide note in the other.

Laura's mother refused to believe the suicide theory for several reasons. First of all, she had just received a cheerful letter from Laura saying she would be home soon for a visit. Mrs. Mathews also found it suspicious that there were no gunpowder burns found on her daughter, and the suicide note looked forged. Mrs. Mathews demanded an inquest, and a coroner's jury was formed. During the spectacular hearing, several strange inconsistencies emerged. For example, detectives learned that Tillie had sent telegrams informing relatives about Laura's suicide without yet knowing her fate. Another surprise happened when police questioned Mr. Coey about Laura Mathews's death and he denied knowing her. When pressed, he explained the little misunderstanding by saying that he called her by her stage name, never her given name. A nosy hotel maid testified that she had read dozens of sappy love letters from Mr. Coey. However, all the letters from the debonair millionaire mysteriously disappeared the day after Laura was found dead. Mr. Rumbaugh was also subpoenaed to court; however, when he did not show up to testify, a warrant was issued for his arrest.

It was eerie when court officers broke into Rumbaugh's hotel room and saw dozens of drawings of the stage actress Laura Mathews staring at them from every wall. Rumbaugh was found lying naked in bed with a picture of Laura on his chest, splattered in blood. There was a bullet hole in his right temple, and brains were oozing out his left ear—but amazingly, the half-brained victim was still alive. Deputies rushed Rumbaugh to the hospital, but he died the next day. A suicide note instructed how to settle his estate and told his mother he was sorry for "doing a terrible thing." Detectives learned that Rumbaugh had been infatuated with Laura Mathews and had been stalking her for two weeks. It was also revealed that he was from a prominent Pennsylvania family and was married with children. Investigators theorized that Rumbaugh might have murdered Laura; however, after his tragic suicide, he was exonerated posthumously from killing the beautiful young actress.

On August 1, 1908, the foreman of the coroner's jury announced:

> *We, the jury find that Laura Mathews came to her death by the shot of a pistol; that said pistol wound was self inflicted with suicide intent after 8:30 o'clock P.M. Sunday July 28, 1908, and took place on the 10th street hill, Ivywild, in El Paso County, state of Colorado.*

Mysteriously, at the very moment the suicide verdict was announced, a haunting high-pitched scream reverberated throughout the building. Janitors thought the boiler had exploded until it was discovered that the timing cable on the courthouse clock had suddenly snapped. Time stood still on the courthouse clock tower for many years until enough money was saved to replace the expensive copper cable. The clock still acts as if is possessed by unseen forces now and then, and paranormal investigators have become convinced that it is a message from the grave of Laura Mathews.

The Acacia Hotel is also said to be haunted by Laura's restless spirit. The old grande dame rents rooms for senior housing and also hosts a beauty parlor, barbershop and, until just a couple years ago, a quaint neighborhood pub called Jinx Place. The little hole in the wall was a local hot spot for artists, writers and actors for decades. The bar was owned by Jinx Clark, a tough-as-nails rancher's daughter and champion figure skater who toured with the Broadmoor Hotel's *Holiday on Ice* show before buying the joint in 1960. No matter what the season, it was always merry at Jinx Place. Foil Christmas trees dressed in multicolored bulbs crowded the bar top, while green tinsel hung from the ceiling like Spanish moss. Every black leatherette booth had a plastic poinsettia centerpiece that seemed to thrive on stale beer and cigarette butts. Jinx won a figure-skating championship on Christmas Eve 1946; her lucky ice skates hung proudly above the cash register adorned with a token sprig of plastic mistletoe.

Local lore told that the bar (now a print shop) was haunted by the legendary actress Laura Mathews. A portrait of Laura was painted by local artist Gail Anne Bailey and hung proudly over the pool table for eons. One Saturday night, a group of costumed performers from a community theater group went to Jinx's after a show. Actor Robert Rais saw a beautiful woman dressed in old-fashioned clothing who looked exactly like the portrait of Laura. He asked the stranger if she was also an entertainer, and she nodded affirmatively and then vanished before his eyes. The startled thespian ran screaming from the building, swearing to never return to the den of horror. When Jinx heard the commotion, she pulled a Saturday night special

The painting of Laura Mathews that once hung in Jinx Place. *Courtesy of Gail Anne Bailey.*

from behind the counter and exclaimed in her deep husky voice, "If that damn ghost scares away any more good paying customers, I'll shoot her!" Then she accidently shot a hole right through the ceiling. About a dozen people scattered, seeking refuge under plastic reindeer and cardboard Santas as chunks of plaster fell from the heavens. Moments later, dazed revelers emerged from the rubble and collected their wits. Covered in dust, grime and silver tinsel, an old barfly slurred, "Jiminy Cricket, Jinx…If that was last call, all you had to do was say so!"

The Pioneer Museum is the pride and joy of Colorado Springs and houses a wealth of information about the Front Range. The museum's gift shop is one of the best resources in town for books about local history. The city-owned museum is open from Tuesday through Saturday and is free to the public, although donations are greatly appreciated.

Haunted Hospitals
of Little London

She just goes a little mad sometimes. We all go a little mad sometimes. Haven't you?
—Norman Bates, Psycho

Hospitals have been called portals for souls coming and going from this world and are considered to be the most haunted places on the planet. Ask any ghost hunter to tell you about a favorite spooky hot spot and she will most likely tell you about a haunted hospital. Most hospital workers can attest to the hauntings, especially those who work the scary graveyard shift. Hospital administrators are well aware that it is difficult to find employees who are willing to work the haunted night shift; therefore, these workers are often compensated with higher wages than their daytime counterparts. Legends of haunted hospitals are known all over the country, and some of these well-worn tales date back as far as the Civil War era. War hospitals were sites of misery, pain and death and were perhaps the first known haunted institutions in the country. Sometimes large homes, like the Canton Mansion in Franklin, Tennessee, were used as makeshift hospitals. This mansion was used as a Confederate hospital during the Battle of Franklin and is well documented as being haunted. Paranormal investigators have recorded sounds of gunshots, explosions, drum beats and battle cries. Strange, unexplainable images of orbs, streaks of light and phantom faces have been photographed in and around the old hospital grounds.

In addition to war hospitals, tuberculosis sanatoriums are also well-known places for paranormal activity. In Chardon, Ohio, a little boy ghost wearing knickers has been seen many times at Heather Hill Hospital. He often runs in and out of rooms, seemingly playing a game of keep-away with awed and speechless spectators. When staff members make chase, he runs into another room, laughing, and then mysteriously disappears. No one knows who the resident ghost is, so he has gone by the name of "Knickers Boy" for many years.

The Pikes Peak region has several haunted hospitals with national notoriety, as well. In Manitou Springs, a former tuberculosis hospital now known as Miramont Castle Museum was once the home of a wealthy Franciscan priest before it was converted into a sanatorium by the Sisters of Mercy. The castle is said to be haunted by several spirits, including the priest, his mother, a suicidal pregnant nun and Jenny the ghost girl. Jenny is often seen bouncing about the gift shop of the museum, and she loves to play in the doll room. A little ghost girl named Shirley haunts neighboring Red Crags Manor. The estate was built by Manitou Springs founding father Dr. William Bell. This mansion was also converted into a tuberculosis sanatorium and is now a bed-and-breakfast. Red Crags is believed to be haunted by at least two former patients, including a soldier who appears on the third floor wearing a tattered military uniform and a beautiful woman in white who is seen wandering the lawn.

Several hospitals were built in Colorado Springs during the town's infancy, when tuberculosis was killing people in droves. Fear of catching the disease became epidemic in itself, and in the late 1880s, Colorado legislators almost passed a bill that would require tuberculosis patients known as "lungers" to wear bells around their necks to indicate that they were infected. Spitting on sidewalks and sharing eating and drinking utensils became taboo. The only known treatment was rest, nutrition, dry air and sunshine. Colorado Springs became a desirable location for lungers because of its ideal climate, and thousands of victims flocked to the city in search of a cure. Many of them became permanent residents. It is baffling to recall today that just eighty years ago one in three citizens suffered from the deadly disease.

At one time, there were seventeen tuberculosis hospitals in the area. The Woodmen of America Sanatorium was a thousand-acre open-air campus in Woodmen Valley that held over two hundred identical teepees designed to isolate patients and allow cool mountain air to circulate around them. Each tent was sparsely furnished with a white iron bed, a table, a chair, a chamber pot, sputum cups and an emergency bell. During blizzards and windstorms, many of these top-heavy tents blew over, leaving barefooted pajama-clad patients to scramble for shelter. Gluttony was strictly enforced; patients

An antique postcard of the old Woodman of America tuberculosis sanatorium. *Author's collection.*

were required to drink at least three liters of whole milk and dozens of raw eggs daily. The goal was for each patient to gain at least twenty pounds during convalescence, which led many to jokingly refer to the camp as "Puke Ranch." The sanatorium closed after forty years of business, and the Sisters of Saint Francis Seraph took over the property in 1954.

Until twenty years ago, Woodman Valley was still just open space, ranch land and the Catholic convent. The hills, meadows and crags were a favorite spot for youngsters to hunt small game, especially jackalopes, a small breed of horned rabbits that are cute, cuddly and, most of all, delicious. In the summer of 1973, a local chapter of boy scouts camped at a ranch in Woodmen Valley for the weekend. While roasting weenies around the campfire, their leader told about a mysterious cemetery at the nearby convent. Mr. Smith filled their hearts with fear as he told tales of glowing graves and suicidal nun zombies that haunted the hillsides. Later that night, Mr. Smith led a few brave boys on a moonlit hike through the cemetery and witnessed millions of colored orbs dancing through the headstones as a cacophony of bells rang. Smith truly believed that they shared a bonafide paranormal experience and quipped that he wished he could honor the kids with a ghost hunter merit badge. Since then, many people have witnessed phantom lights and mysterious chiming in Woodman Valley and believe that the ghosts of diseased lungers still haunt the area to this day.

Another haunted hospital stands as the former YWCA building on the corner of Nevada Avenue and Kiowa Street. Believe it or not, the lovely five-story building with its Van Briggle pottery façade was converted into a Red Cross hospital during the Spanish influenza crisis of 1918. Next door to the makeshift hospital was an undertaking establishment that became saturated with business during the pandemic. Stiffs were stacked sky high, so the overflow had to be stuffed into the basement of the Red Cross hospital. The old makeshift morgue is now a popular nightclub known as the Underground Bar. Owner Jerry Morris believes that the historic building is haunted because employees sometimes complain that they feel an unseen force watching them, especially when they are alone in the kitchen at night. Colorado Ghost Tours confirmed that the building is haunted when it placed recording devices in an area known as "The Pit" and got several good EVP readings of disembodied voices. A man's voice can be heard saying, "Help me!" and another is heard moaning.

The Colorado Springs Psychopathic Hospital (now called Cedar Springs) has been known to be haunted ever since it was built. The first report of ghostly activity happened shortly after the hospital opened in 1923. That same year, a mental patient began shooting his pistol into imaginary phantoms because he said that the Indian spirits buried there ordered him to do so. Rumors began to swirl that the hospital was built on ancient Indian burial grounds, and folks began prowling the property at night in hope of seeing hellish apparitions.

The best-known ghost of the mental hospital is said to be Farmer Floyd, a suicide victim who has been haunting the campus for over sixty years. The story goes that the thirty-eight-year-old bachelor fell madly in love with his forty-year-old divorced housekeeper named Lois. Not a day went by that Floyd didn't ask the pretty Hispanic woman to marry him. According to her eighteen-year-old daughter, the redneck fell in love with her mother and was a great guy until he went on a bender. Sometimes his drunken binges lasted for weeks, and Lois often feared for her life but stayed with the bully because she believed she could do no better. Finally, after eight years of torture, Lois got fed up and left the drunkard in December 1947.

Luck was with Lois, and she swiftly got a job as head housekeeper at the Colorado Springs Psychopathic Hospital. The position paid well, had good benefits and included a cozy apartment above the laundry room with a beautiful view of the park-like grounds below. The newly independent woman believed her whereabouts were secret until Floyd came knocking on her door nine months later. After she refused his final wedding proposal, Floyd pulled a pistol from his pocket and shot Lois through the heart. He then pierced his own with a bullet as well. The press noticed the symbolic gesture, and newspaper articles across the country featured stories about the star-crossed lovers. The photos taken of the murder scene haunted folks for many years. The forlorn farmer and his Mexican Chiquita were shown sprawled in a pool of blood on a wooden floor. Floyd held a gun in one hand and an engagement ring in the other. To add to the tragedy, a love letter written by the farmer was found in the housekeeper's apron pocket. It proclaimed true love for the Hispanic woman, saying, "Life without you would be unbearable," and it implored her to move back to the *hacienda*. The smitten farmer promised to do anything to win back her love, including giving up the bottle and tearing down his beloved backyard still. He even sweetened the deal by promising to buy her a new vacuum cleaner and washing machine. The letter was dated September 8, 1948. Sadly, just four days later, Lois's daughter discovered the murder-suicide.

The first indication that the caretaker's apartment was haunted came when the bloodstain could not be erased no matter how many times it was covered with paint. The floor was even sanded and primed, but the blemish kept bleeding through. Rumors began circulating about the haunted hospital, and the ghost stories spread far beyond its well-manicured lawns. Years later, after the mental hospital became known as Brady's, it was considered a rite of passage for high school seniors to run through the campus naked on graduation night. Another dare was to drive to Brady's on a full moon night and wait for the ghost of Farmer Floyd to appear. There were countless stories about the ghostly farmer throwing rocks at amorous teenagers making out in the parking lot. The haunted mental hospital became so popular on Friday and Saturday nights that an eight-foot-tall fence was installed around the property to keep trespassing teeny boppers at bay. The concept seems rather bizarre today since most mental institutions have fences to prevent escape rather than to keep people out.

Over the years, many people have seen the ghost of the farmer haunting the grounds of the hospital. He is said to look so lifelike that many have confused him for a maintenance worker; however, he has become identifiable by his bloodstained denim overalls. Talk around the water trough is that Farmer Floyd will continue to haunt the hospital until he finally realizes that he bought the farm—a long, long time ago.

SHADES OF THE MAYOR'S MANSION
AND PIONEER PARK

"Over the Mountains of the Moon, Down the Valley of the Shadow, Ride, boldly ride," the Shade replied, "if you seek for Eldorado."
—*Edgar Allan Poe, 1849*

If the ancient stone walls and brick pathways of Old Colorado City could talk, we would surely hear all kinds of fanciful stories about Indian raids, Civil War heroes, bootleggers, soiled doves, outlaw renegades and a couple spooky ghost stories as well. Colorado City was one of the first towns established in the new provisional territory of Kansas and got its start as a hub for the Pikes Peak or Bust gold rush in 1859. Thousands of hopeful miners seeking the legendary riches of Eldorado stormed into the region. Founder Anthony Bott had high hopes that politicians would declare Colorado City the state capital, but the honor was eventually bestowed on Denver instead. However, all was not lost because Colorado City soon became famous for more notorious reasons.

Shortly after Colorado Springs was established in 1874, founding father and conservative general Palmer declared that Colorado Springs would be "dry," making drinking, buying or selling alcohol strictly forbidden. Thirsty cowboys had to wet their whistles just west of Fountain Creek in what was already beginning to be called "Old Town." Within just a few years, over twenty bars and gambling houses lined the south side of Colorado Avenue. A popular bar known as the Bucket of Blood hung its shingle near Twenty-fifth Street, and notorious outlaws Bob Ford and Cole Younger played faro at the nearby Crystal Palace gambling hall. Secret tunnels led to whorehouses and underground opium dens, allowing discretion for particular customers. Outlaw activity in Old Town was so rampant that it soon became known as a veritable Sodom and Gomorrah.

Ghost stories about Colorado City started being told shortly after the town opened its doors, and some of the earliest were about the El Paso House. The two-story building was built to replace a smaller lodge on the corner of Twenty-eighth Street and Colorado Avenue in 1860. The twelve-bedroom hotel had all the comforts of home, including an unprecedented extra outhouse built especially for visiting politicians. Old-timers say that the mansion attracted many famous guests, including former president Teddy Roosevelt, politician William Jennings Bryan and the notorious outlaw Jesse James. The infamous hotel was rumored to be haunted almost from its very beginning when one of the builders, George Smith, was murdered in an Indian raid in the San Juan Mountains. Shortly after the attack, Smith's gruesome-looking ghost was seen wandering the hallways—without a scalp. When Colorado territorial legislators learned that the inn was haunted, they were said to be afraid of both the hairless ghost roaming around inside the hotel *and* the Indian warriors camped outside on the lawn.

Generally speaking, relationships with the American Indian tribes were peaceful; sometimes, however, tensions were strained, like when a pioneer family in Monument was brutally attacked by Indians. The savages ripped an unborn child from the womb of a Mrs. Hungate, and she was found dead along with the rest of her family near the smoldering ashes of their homestead. When word reached Colorado City about the vicious attack, heated talks led to a call to arms, and volunteers were asked to join the crusade against the savage Indians. Men from all around the region met at the El Paso House to join the third militia who camped there after their recent Civil War victory at Glorietta Pass. One of these fine young men was twenty-year-old Leon Murat, a handsome Frenchman who was secretly engaged to Maria Tinville. Maria begged her lover not to leave, but he heard Colonel Chivington's call to duty, and he was determined to do what was honorable. However, he promised his fiancée that he would come back a hero and that they would marry as soon as he returned from Sand Creek.

The night before Leon Murat was to leave for battle, Maria stole some money and a horse from her parents and fled to the El Paso House, where Chivington's troops were camped. She kissed her lover and bid him a tearful farewell, promising to be there waiting for him when he returned. Guests later told of how the young girl never left her room during her entire stay at the El Paso House because she was fearful of her scorned father. Finally, word came that Murat was killed on the battlefield, and Maria went insane with grief. Like a man without a country, the young girl was without a home; her lover was dead, and her parents refused her return. Legend tells that the distraught young woman left the hotel and wandered the hillsides stricken with madness. Sadly, her corpse was found frozen on the banks of Fountain Creek behind the El Paso House a few months later, and the poor girl was buried on top of the mesa.

Not long after, the ghost of Maria Tinville was seen walking along Fountain Creek, as well as near her grave. Amazingly, her mournful phantom was even reported nearly half a century after her death, and the ghost story of the tragic young lovers was published in the *Colorado Springs Gazette* on December 11, 1904, with the caption:

STRANGE PHENOMENA SEEN AT LONELY GRAVE ON THE MESA

High upon the mesa northwest of Colorado City, near the old cemetery used by the pioneers of the sixties, there is a lone grave ground to which clings a romance of early days which is recalled by like phenomena, which many persons say they have witnessed when passing by at night.

As the story goes, Marie Tinville, beautiful daughter of Victor Tinville, lived with her parents in a cabin near Colorado City in 1863. About that time Leon Murat, a dashing young fellow of about 20 years old came out from Saint Louis and found employment on her father's ranch. It was a case of love at first sight, intensified by isolated conditions and an almost constant companionship.

Love's young dream was rudely awakened in the autumn of 1864 in a call to arms by Colonel Chivington in his campaign against the hostile Indian. Men were needed and Leon was brave. He kissed his sweetheart a hurried goodbye and rode away with that avenging column of horsemen. A few weeks later, the battle at sand creek was fought and the young lover was killed upon the battle field. When the news of the death reached Maria she fell into a swoon after which her mind became a blank. From that time on her decline was rapid and in a few months she was laid in a lonely grave upon the mesa.

After that, stories were told of strange things, a white light was seen close to the grave which vanished upon approach. Once old Ben Johnson came to town at night with his long hair fairly on end, and said that a white light had risen in front of him near the grave out of which protruded a naked arm. The incredulous asked him what he had been drinking but he stuck to the story as long as he lived.

These stories were revived some time ago and the other night out of curiosity, W.A. Brittel paid a visit to the grave. He saw a white light the same moment felt a touch on his cheek that stung like an electric shock. Birdsall (the town Sheriff) thought it all a joke and went out a night or two afterwards. No white light, but felt a peculiarly cold air and the touch on his cheek as soft as if someone had kissed him.

According to legend, the ghost of Leon Murat was also seen haunting the El Paso House shortly after his death. Several guests, as well as employees, claimed to see the ghost of the young, handsome cowboy wandering the halls and grounds of the hostelry and even heard him calling for his beloved Maria.

A few years later, the hotel was believed to also be haunted by the spirit of Charles Stockbridge, who bought the El Paso House in 1874. The former hotel was the only house around big enough to accommodate his clan, which included his wife and their thirteen children. Soon after purchasing the house, Stockbridge built the El Paso County Brewing Company, and a secret tunnel leading to it, across the street from his home. Underground

The Stockbridge House. *Courtesy of Leasures Treasures.*

hiding rooms that were used during Indian attacks were also used to store booze and became known as the whiskey caves. Stockbridge was said to be a friend and drinking buddy to the Indians; in fact, Chief Colorow often traded with the booze peddler to procure firewater. Supplying alcohol to the Indians was illegal, but to whom could the townsfolk complain since the good-time Charlie was also the first mayor of the town?

Charles Stockbridge was accused of peddling whiskey bottled as cough medicine in his Colorado Springs drugstore and for selling spiked milkshakes from the apothecary soda fountain—much to the dismay of fellow statesman and teetotaler General Palmer. It wasn't long before the boozehound acquired an unsavory reputation, especially after folks at the Baptist church complained that he had reneged on donations and other campaign promises. It seems that Charles Stockbridge lived by his own rules, and his attitude earned him a few enemies around town. Some of these men tried to burn down his house, not just once but twice, and finally succeeded on New Year's Eve 1890. However, the arson attacks only made the portly politician more fiercely determined to hold his ground. On New Year's Day, Mayor Stockbridge stood on top of the smoldering ashes of the El Paso House and shook his clenched fist at the heavens, declaring that his new home would be a fortress that "neither fire, nor hail, nor wrath could destroy."

The new Mayor's Mansion was built over the rubble with thick stone walls and a fireproof copper roof. An elaborate wrought-iron widow's walk was added so that Stockbridge could peer from the rooftop with shotgun in hand and gaze over his hard-won empire. The expansive lawns were decorated with elaborate wrought-iron fencing, statues and a pond where the local kids liked to fish for minnows, frogs and crawdads. Newspaper articles raved about the spectacular parties held at the Mayor's Mansion, and it was soon considered to be the cornerstone of the community.

One of the biggest social gatherings was hosted at the El Paso House on November 29, 1899, when folks came from all over the region to pay their last respects at the funeral of Charles Stockbridge, who died of alcoholism at the ripe old age of fifty-five. Not long after, his merry widow ran off with a gambler from Pueblo who blew all her inheritance at the racetrack, and she was sadly forced to sell the beloved mansion. Over the years, rumors about the Stockbridge estate being haunted persisted. Many citizens claim to have seen the shadowy apparition of the stout mayor watching over his mansion with shotgun in hand, pacing the rooftop widow's walk just as he once did long ago.

Mrs. Stockbridge dressed in all her finery. *Courtesy of Leasures Treasures.*

When Elden and Sylvia Leasure bought the old Stockbridge House in 1979, the previous owner warned them that the mansion was haunted, but they were not deterred by the silly rumors because it suited their needs perfectly. The Amarillo Motel was built on the old campground behind the mansion in 1948 and provided welcome additional income for the couple. The family moved into the upstairs quarters of the historic building while their business, Leasures Treasures, was operated from the main level. The home was in need of a few repairs, and the couple set off at once to conquer the task. Fortunately, the beautiful woodwork throughout the historic mansion was in good condition; however, all of the historic wallpaper was painted a lovely shade of army green. One time, Sylvia told her husband that she wished she knew what the original wallpaper looked like, and the next day a large painting left hanging on the wall by the former owners had somehow moved to reveal a rectangular patch of the original unpainted wallpaper. Other mysteries were revealed during restoration, including a hidden staircase leading to the widow's walk and also an underground tunnel that was sealed off but once led to the secret whiskey caves.

Several other unexplainable strange things happened over the years, particularly in an upstairs bedroom where two of the Stockbridge daughters died of pneumonia. Mysterious cold spots were often felt in that bedroom, and the Leasures' dog was afraid to go in there as well. Laughter and music has also been heard in that same room when no one is present. The strangest thing that ever happened to Elden was when he saw the apparition of a cowboy wearing blue jeans and a checkered shirt walk across the room and disappear. He said what was really spooky about the experience is that he was the only one in the building and all the doors were deadbolted from the inside. Could this be the ghost of Charles Stockbridge or perhaps young Leon Murat?

The Leasures confirmed that the haunting in the building settled down not long after the renovations were completed in 1985. Perhaps Charles Stockbridge likes having the Leasures for company because he, too, was an avid gun collector. Leasures Treasures is a history lover's dream with an extensive collection of antique guns, as well as glass cases overflowing with historical gems. Elden has sought out military memorabilia his entire life, and his wife—also an avid collector—has a fondness for meat grinders. Someone should call Guinness to see what the world record is because Sylvia Leasure just might be a contender. The former schoolteacher is proud to own over fifty models of the hand-cranked kitchen tool. On second thought, it might be better to call Ripley's because a larger collection of meat grinders anywhere would definitely be hard to believe.

Elden and Sylvia are a delightful couple who have been in business for fifty years and are only the fourth owners of the historic Mayor's Mansion on Colorado Avenue. If you are ever in that neck of the woods, be sure to stop in and say hi. The Leasures' and their staff are always happy to share their extensive knowledge of antiques (especially military memorabilia and meat grinders), as well as stories about the famous historic landmark building.

Meanwhile, up on the mesa, the luminous ghost of Maria Tinville still haunts her grave—which is somewhere near third base. She has also been seen sashaying by the monkey bars, as well as sitting on a tire swing. Perhaps Maria is upset because her final resting place has become a public park. The Mesa Cemetery is now known as Pioneer Park, and it is located off Panorama Drive and Frontier Street on Fillmore Hill. The last burial there occurred in 1907, and soon after the property fell into a state of disrepair. In 1973, a survey was conducted using sonar equipment, and it was determined that at least 250 unmarked graves were still buried beneath the eight-acre parcel. Finally, the city decided to turn the old cemetery into a memorial park with a granite marker commemorating all the pioneers still buried six feet under. Sod covered the former graveyard, playground equipment was installed and if it weren't for the historical marker, no one would know about the park's buried secrets…or of the ghosts that have been left behind.

DARK SECRETS OF FOUNTAIN AND THE HOVENA HOUSE

The communication of the dead is tongued with fire beyond the language of the living.
—*T.S. Eliot*

S ome people might think that Fountain is a suburb of Colorado Springs, but it is in fact its own town established years before others in El Paso County. Fountain residents are very proud of its heritage and have certainly earned bragging rights; in 1999, the town was designated as the "Millennium City of the United States" by the *New York Times*. An even bigger honor was heaped on the railroad hub in 2002, when it was awarded the title "All-America City" by the National Civic League. The town of Fountain has been synonymous with Halloween ever since 1936, when the Venetucci family opened their farm to children for an annual pumpkin giveaway. However, the hamlet had a spooky reputation long before the pumpkin patch was planted or even before the town had a name. Therefore, some ghost hunters have added another distinguished title to the list of honors and have declared Fountain, Colorado, an "All-America Haunted City" as well.

At first, the hub was just a little prairie trading post known as Jimmy Camp that was plopped in the middle of Ute hunting grounds. Building in a bad neighborhood had its disadvantages, and the community was subjugated to many terrorist attacks. On October 13, 1841, a stagecoach en route from Colorado City was robbed of $40,000 near the trading post. Several Indians were killed during the robbery and later buried on a hill near Rock Creek. The rock-ringed graves can still be seen on the mesa and beg the question:

why would the stagecoach drivers go to the trouble of burying the dead savages and marking their graves? Rumor says that after the Indians were killed, they were discovered to be white men in disguise, so the scoundrels were given a decent Christian burial. Legend also says that the stagecoach drivers hid the cache of gold inside the graves, hoping to steal it later. But the conniving opportunists were killed before they could claim their prize, and the treasure remains buried there to this day. Could the dark shadow that patrols the hilltop at night be a supernatural being protecting a buried treasure? Many folks in Fountain think so because the lurking shadow has been seen ever since the burials took place on the mesa long ago.

A haunted drive in Fountain is the Old Pueblo Road, which was once the stagecoach route. The historic lane laces through the countryside where old homesteads can still be seen dotting the grassy hill and dale. Local legend tells about a hanging tree on the road where several horse thieves were lynched. On full moon nights, ghosts of the dead banditos can be seen swinging by their heads from lofty tree branches. Many deadly car and train accidents have occurred on the old forgotten road, which runs

The Devil's Perch on the old Pueblo Road. *Courtesy of the SpiritChasers.*

parallel with the train tracks. In 1888, several people died when a train car full of dynamite exploded, sending shrapnel through the air for miles, and a thunderous jolt was felt from Monument to Lamar. A railroad bridge known as the Devil's Perch is especially haunted; not only have several accidents happened there but a few suicides as well. Times were tough in the olden days, and several ranchers leapt from the twin trellises in search of greener pastures. Mysteriously, screams can still sometimes be heard coming from the Devil's Perch late at night when absolutely no one is around.

Tucked on the corner of Old Pueblo Road and Illinois Street is an old decrepit antebellum mansion that looks like a miniature version of Tara from the book *Gone With the Wind*. The mansion was a brothel for many years until it was sold to a strange old lady whom locals called the "Goat Woman." Edith Halcomb earned the moniker because she often paraded around town wearing just a bathrobe while leading a pack of horned billy goats as if she were the Pied Piper. The eccentric Goat Woman ran an antique shop on the main level of the dilapidated manor and a secret abortion clinic in the basement until she was prosecuted and thrown in the slammer. The home has had several owners, and many of them complained that their abode was haunted—especially by menacing phantom faces lurking in the fireplace. Perhaps its spooky reputation is why the once stately home has sat on the market for years. However, the Goat Woman's antebellum abode was not always the most ghost-riddled place in Fountain; up until just a few years ago, that dubious distinction belonged to a mysterious mansion on El Paso Street known as the Hovena House.

The Hovena House was built as a wedding gift for a beautiful and spirited woman named Hovena Lock. (Hovena was given her lyrical name by her father, who was a fan of famed composer Ludwig van Beethoven.) The stately mansion was built with thick rock walls and was used as a fort by the early pioneers during Indian raids. Sadly, a friend of Hovena's was scalped on the back lawn when she could not reach the shelter before one of the deadly attacks.

Over the years, the historic manor fell into a saddened state of decay, perhaps because of the shame that was harbored within its keep. The secret buried there festered for over a century and slowly consumed the home like a cancer until it was cut from the walls and the mystery of the old haunted mansion was finally solved.

The story begins with John W. Spicer, the youngest of twelve children born on a rural farm in Michigan. When his mother died, the nineteen-year-old greenhorn left home in search of happy trails and became a cowboy in Texas. He lived in the saddle for three long years, and like many other cowpokes on the Chisholm Trail, he took up the harmonica, as well as drinking, to comfort a lonesome heart. In 1885, the bowlegged cowboy had enough of the hard living, so he hung up his spurs, put down the bottle and moved to Denver in search of a brighter tomorrow. Spicer stayed there for a year and acquired carpentry skills; then he took the stagecoach to booming Fountain Valley with hope of plying his new trade. As the coach neared the stage stop, John Spicer got so excited at seeing the Fountain Valley Saloon that he threw off his cowboy hat and cheered, "Yee-haw!" Bystanders were dismayed when he then slipped and fell off the wagon. It took several days for Spicer to recover from a twisted ankle—and a horrible hangover. It seems that the cowboy-carpenter was so excited about moving from Denver to the valley that he brought a bottle of whiskey and celebrated along the way. Folks at the saloon teased the former teetotaler, quipping that he fell off the wagon in more ways than one when he arrived in town drunk as a skunk that day.

John Spicer proved to be a highly skilled carpenter, despite his proclivity for drink. His claim to fame were custom-built tip-out flour bins, and his talent was much sought after. A year later, he was hired by a wealthy rancher named Mr. Loomis, who became his mentor, and the cowboy-carpenter soon swore off booze and found religion. It was at the Free Methodist Church that John Spicer met a rich man's daughter named Hovena Lock, whose family was one of the first clans to settle in the valley. When John first laid eyes on the young woman, he thought she was cuter than a speckled pup under a red wagon and was heartbroken when he heard she was engaged. One day, Hovena had a horseback-riding date with her fiancé, but he failed to meet her at the church as planned. Fate stepped in when Spicer happened to be there that Sunday afternoon and went riding with her instead. Six months later, John Spicer and Hovena Lock were married. Sadly, the groom started celebrating with a wedding toast, and what really takes the cake is that he never stopped.

Most of the time, John Spicer did his boozing at a shack that he built on Fountain Creek. His "clubhouse" was where he brewed homemade moonshine and drank with bad company while his wife and their six children kept the home fires burning. Occasionally, he sobered up long enough to get a carpentry job, or he would work on a nearby ranch breaking wild horses, but mostly the drunkard lived off the Lock family name and inheritance. Opportunity knocked on John Spicer's door in 1901, after he started a guide business and was hired by Vice President Theodore Roosevelt to lead a

Hovena and John Spicer on their wedding day. *Courtesy of Dean and Penny Cimino.*

"bear-hunting party." However, all glory was lost when the disillusioned warriors returned without a kill because Spicer only heard "Party!" and drank the entire week they were gone. All the boozehound could say about the embarrassing fiasco was: "Some days you eat the bear…and other days the bear eats you."

John Spicer's drinking only got worse as the years dragged by, and on their twentieth wedding anniversary, he went on a bender and attempted to kill Hovena and their youngest son. The raging maniac had brutalized his wife on several occasions, but this was the first time he ever attacked one of the children, and Hovena was determined to make it the last. The next morning, John Spicer didn't remember a thing when he woke up staring into the barrel of a shotgun. As he scrambled down the driveway, Hovena sent a bullet after him and screamed, "I swear by all that is holy that if you ever step foot in this valley again, John Spicer, I will blow your fool head off!" And that was the last time she ever saw her deadbeat hubby. Fortunately, Hovena lived peacefully in the home that Spicer built for her until she died of old age in 1938.

Shortly after Hovena died, her former home developed a haunted reputation and sat empty until it became the Mayor's Mansion in 1942. A few years later, it was turned into an apartment building, and the spooky tales about the building grew wickeder as the years went by. Doors and windows would open and slam shut at all hours, and an incessant internal tapping was heard coming from the walls. Different owners over the years complained about the "bad vibes," and the historic home went through a slew of owners, especially after the paranormal activity became aggressive. One former tenant said that she lived there for a week and left with just a suitcase after pots and pans went flying across the kitchen. Because of its spooky reputation, keeping renters was a futile challenge, especially after the home fell into a terrible unkempt condition. Sadly, the once glorious estate was targeted for the wrecking ball until a young family intervened and bought the dilapidated mansion for a song and prayer in 1985.

When the new owners moved into the haunted abode, they immediately began experiencing all kinds of strange paranormal activity, especially when they started remodeling; however, they tried to shrug it off because they did not want to frighten their children. In May 1986, the family was working together to gut an upstairs bedroom when the oldest child noticed pencil marks scrawled inside a piece of old wood molding. The handwriting was smeared in some places but was still legible, and the family waited in suspense as the shocking letter was read out loud:

> *To whoever should happen to find this confession, I John W. Spicer of the city of Fountain, state of Colorado bring about this shuffle of mortal coil to make this my full confession in hope that when I am gone it may be found and at last clear up the darkest murder that ever embraced one in human murder. On or about the* [illegible] *day of March 1893, some four miles north of this city, and two miles east of the foot of Cheyenne Mountain, I did willfully kill and* [illegible] *murder with a club one John J. Sebastian for his money and his jewelry worth $5,000 and did drag the mutilated body to a deep ravine some 500 yards distance from the point already mentioned in my confession then* [illegible] *his lonely last* [illegible] *bring about to die* [illegible] *find the retribution that awaits here in the world to come are spending my last moments in prayer for the partial salvation of my soul.*

The family promptly called the *Gazette* newspaper thinking that it would be interested in the mystery; however, the receptionist just heard "murder confession" and promptly called the police. Ten minutes later, three squad cars pulled up in front of the mansion with veteran homicide detectives demanding answers. Deputies wrapped the property in bright yellow crime scene tape and turned the mansion upside down looking for further clues. Detectives worked with historians and discovered that there was a Mr. John J. Sebastian who was a resident of Fountain in the early 1890s, but he mysteriously disappeared after going on a hunting trip with John Spicer. One of Spicer's daughters was found living in Pueblo and almost suffered from heart failure when homicide detectives came knocking on her door. At first, the old woman refused to cooperate and even became hostile, but she relented a few days later saying she had a change of heart and that it was time for the truth to be told. She admitted that her father was a "real bastard when he was drinking" and recalled that during a brief time in her childhood her family seemed

Dean and Penny Cimino with the murder confession. *Courtesy of the Fountain Museum.*

to have come into a lot of money, but it didn't last long because of her father's alcoholism.

The Cimino family has owned the Hovena House since 1994, and when I contacted them for an interview about their haunted mansion, Mrs. Penny Cimino joked, "What took you so long? I always knew that there was a ghost story here, just begging to be told!" She explained that the house came up for sale when they weren't even looking to buy, but they fell in love with it the moment they stepped over the threshold. A contract had already been placed on the house, but they wanted it so bad that they offered full price. She said they felt drawn to the home for some strange reason but figured it was just because they were both history buffs. However, the couple found it rather eerie when they discovered that they shared the same wedding date with the Spicers—exactly one hundred years later! When the Ciminos bought the old estate, the secret in the wall had already been exposed. However, the mansion still had a haunted feeling about it, and Penny Cimino thought she knew why. John Spicer's confession was still held captive in the district attorney's cold case file, even though the murder was committed over one hundred years ago. She requested that the wood molding be returned to her home, but the district attorney refused, claiming that unsolved murder cases are never closed. After seven years of wrangling, the state's evidence was finally given to the Fountain City Museum after Penny and Dean signed a waiver releasing the property to the historical society. The couple and their teenage sons, Nathaniel and Jeremy, are glad that John Spicer's secret can now be shared by all and are relieved that their formerly haunted home is now at peace.

Ironically, the spooky happenings in the old mansion stopped as soon as John Spicer's murder confession was placed in the town's museum. Could this just be a coincidence? The Ciminos don't think so and are glad that they went the extra mile to put the secret letter back where it should be, where history buffs, armchair detectives and ghost hunters can see it. The plank of wood scrawled with the dark confession just might have solved the oldest cold case in the world. If having the macabre piece of evidence gives the little town of Fountain some additional notoriety, then that makes everyone happy—maybe even the ghosts.

The Fountain Valley Historical Society founded the town museum, which is staffed by dozens of dedicated volunteers. Elaine MacKay has written a book about the history of the valley, and Betty Powell has organized volumes of newspaper articles about the area. Copies of the police investigation are available for purchase in the bookstore, as well as all kinds of interesting antiques, gems and tidbits. The Fountain Valley Museum is located at 114 North Main Street and is free to the public. While in Fountain, make sure to stop at the pink house on Santa Fe Avenue called Cimino Sales. Dean Cimino would be happy to sell you a used car, assist you with any hunting needs or answer any questions you might have about the infamous secret of the Hovena House. Please remember that the Hovena House is a private residence, and trespassing on the property is strictly prohibited.

PIONEER PHANTOMS
AND THE BLACK FOREST

Because I could not stop for Death,
He kindly stopped for me;
The carriage held but just ourselves
and Immortality.
—*Emily Dickinson*

Not many things are scarier than urban sprawl, and Colorado Springs has oozed far beyond its original boundaries, slurping up everything in its path much like the Blob (an alien-amoeba creature of science fiction fame). Few people realize that the city is actually composed of several other little cow towns that were absorbed in the name of progress. Towns like Ivywild, Roswell, Ramona and Old Colorado City were just a few. As the city's hunger grew, it swallowed ranch lands, farms and everything else in its ravenous reach. Sometimes historical indications of the city's early history can still be seen peeking through the urban sprawl. For example, a barnyard looks like a misfit sitting at the intersection of Fillmore and Temple Gap but was there long before the city swelled in that direction. The old homestead has sat next to a nursing home, church and convenience store for years and still does, although the resident donkey has finally gone on to greener pastures.

Living on the prairie was a hard life for pioneering families; not only was the land challenging to cultivate, but also marauding Indians were always a threat. After these so-called savages were murdered and chased away, fence lines were drawn, and the infamous ranch wars began. Historical archives have documented countless murders and "accidental" deaths that occurred on the Colorado range during the 1800s, and no doubt many more went unnoted. Someone was always inadvertently drowning in a water trough after a dispute or accidentally falling down a well. Most of these deadly arguments were over stolen livestock, water or grazing rights. The lawless prairies spawned some of the earliest ghost stories, and one of the first that was published was in the *Gazette Telegraph* on September 24, 1904. It was headlined:

> *GHOST STORIES AT FIRST HAND; THE PHANTOM HORSE AND CARRIAGE*
> *Have you ever read Kipling's' "Phantom Rickshaw"? If so you will be doubly interested in Sundays' Gazette of a phantom horse and buggy in El Paso County.*

The story reported on the apparition of a horse and buggy seen rolling over the prairie roads at rapid speed as a cloud of dust billowed in its wake. Fearful hounds howled, and horses reared in terror as the ghostly image passed silently by. The spooky apparition was first seen by a preacher and his son, who lived on a farm east of Colorado Springs, but was later observed by several other folks, as well. Some witnesses suspected that the strange sight had to do with a pioneer family ambushed and killed by the Indians years earlier. The story goes that the farming family tried to outrun the Indian warriors, but the horse and buggy were no match. Over a century later, the frightening phantom horse and buggy can still be seen late at night rolling silently over the hillsides and kicking up clouds of dust on Drenon Road, even though the old farm lane has been paved for years.

American Indian legends told of ghostly dog soldiers that haunted the prairies seeking vengeance on the white man for the massacre at nearby Sand Creek. Dog soldiers were a fearless group of renegades who reigned with terror over the region during the Indian wars. Their haunting apparitions were often seen riding along the banks of Sand Creek on full moon nights, and rumors about the dead savages haunting the prairie became almost as scary as threats from living Indians.

Another spooky Indian legend was about skin walkers. These ancient supernatural beings ripped skin from their victims and then cloaked themselves with it in order to shape-shift into a new life form. Animals were most often used by these mystical warriors, as cows, horses and other barnyard critters were often found dead in pastures, suspiciously missing their hides. Farmers and ranchers were perplexed when their livestock was strangely brutalized, and even more unnerving was that the flesh from the slaughtered animals was not eaten from the carcasses. Ranchers noticed that coyotes, buzzards and other scavengers refused to dine on the easy pickings, and the mystery concerned many, especially after an unknown man and woman were found on a dirt road stripped of all skin yet fully clothed. The puzzle was never solved, but many people were convinced that the skin walkers were to blame.

The Santa Fe Trail near the Air Force Academy rambles over seventeen miles between Colorado Springs and Palmer Lake. The historic trail was once used by the railroad and laces through several old ghost towns; it is now enjoyed by walkers, runners, historians and paranormal enthusiasts. The area has long been referred to as the Devil's Triangle because of the deadly Indian raids, train accidents and unsolved murders that occurred there, as well as its strange weather patterns. In fact, the windy conditions and rapid weather changes in the area are why the Air Force Academy chose the locale to train pilots. In the late 1800s, gale-force winds blew a train right off the tracks near the town of Husted; fortunately, no one was killed in this accident. However, just a few years later, a dozen other people were not as lucky when two trains collided on August 14, 1909, and landed in a ditch near the same spot. Nine people were instantly killed, and three more died days later. Fifty-nine people were injured, and the fatal wreck was remembered as one of the deadliest train accidents in the state's history. Just days after the horrific accident, folks began talking about the crash site being jinxed and claimed to see ghostly apparitions running in flames down the

A ghost orb startles hikers on the Santa Fe Trail. *Courtesy of Colorado Ghost Tours LLC.*

track screaming for help, and the putrid smell of burning flesh was said to be awful. Some people even went crazy and were emotionally traumatized for years afterward. The *Gazette* published one story about an unfortunate victim on May 28, 1911, that was headlined:

MEXICAN RUNS NUDE FOR THREE DAYS; MILK FROM COWS ONLY NOURISHMENT
Believed to be demented a Mexican giving his name as Jesus Fernandez and who is said to have been running about nude for the last three days in the area of Husted was arrested by the sheriff's office late yesterday afternoon and lodged in the county jail here.

The article went on to say that Jesus Fernandez was taken into custody by the sheriff's office after a telegraph operator in Husted alerted the authorities about the deranged Latino running amok in the countryside. The naked, starving man was suffering from dementia, frostbite and lacerations on his feet and hands when he was caught in the utterly embarrassing act of trying to extrapolate nutrition from a bull. However, after he was fed a hot meal and treated for frostbite, he was peacefully taken to the state mental hospital in Pueblo to be evaluated.

The old town site of Edgerton near the Air Force Academy is a paranormal playground for ghost hunters. The hamlet was established as a stage stop in the 1860s and comprised a post office, general store and the Edgerton Hotel. The little hub was eventually forced to shutter its doors after the Kearney Ranch murders. After all, who wants to stay in a hotel where an axe-wielding maniac is on the loose? The horrific murders are still remembered as some of the most mysterious unsolved crimes in Colorado's history, and the haunting spirits that remain there have long been known to old-timers.

Mrs. Kearney and her six-year-old grandson, James Hand, were living alone on a ranch near Edgerton while the boy's widowed mother was on an extended trip to Boston. On the morning of March 29, 1886, Mrs. Kearney and James delivered baskets filled with painted Easter eggs to their neighbors in the little town of Edgerton. That was the last anyone ever saw the old woman and her cherished grandson alive. Days later, Mrs. Kearney's daughter went to pay her mother a visit and was puzzled when she did not answer the front door. A thick swarm of flies drew her attention to the tackle shed, where the door was splintered and dangling from its hinges. While peering inside, she was horrified to discover her mother's brutalized corpse with a hatchet still lodged in her scalp. The battered body of her eight-year-

A phantom head floating above a horse and buggy near Edgerton. *Courtesy of Gail Anne Bailey.*

old nephew was found stuffed inside a grain bin nearby—another innocent victim of the mysterious killer.

Inside the Kearney ranch house, three dishes were placed on the kitchen table next to a vase of wilted wildflowers. Little black sugar ants had laid claim to a couple cherry pies, and a pot of tomato soup was swimming with yellow maggots. El Paso County deputies were summoned, and robbery was immediately ruled out as a motive. Authorities never discovered who the guest of honor was on that fateful afternoon but reasoned that the ungracious visitor was most likely the killer. Not long after the murders, several people claimed to see the strange transparent apparition of the grandmother and her grandson carrying Easter baskets down the dirt road in Edgerton. News of the haunting spread like wildfire, and folks became afraid to visit the little stage stop. Not long after the horrific murders, the doors of Edgerton were shuttered forever. Today, all that remains are a few historical markers and a haunting ghost story.

Directly across from Edgerton is the district of Black Forest. This region is without a doubt the most haunted area in El Paso County. Even the name "Black Forest" sends shivers down your spine. Ancient lodgepole pines covered the dense, dark hills, so the area was called the "Great Pinery" by early pioneers. Once its haunting reputation was established, a more suitable name was warranted, and folks began calling the area Black Forest. Long ago, the forest was a popular Indian hunting ground that had a migration path coursing through it known as the Cherokee Trail. The Indian path was later used as a stagecoach road during the California gold rush. Then the land was divided and sold into ranch land and logging mills; illegal gin mills were also very popular, and "mountain dew" flowed freely from the hillsides like wine from the Shrine of Baucus. Outlaw activity in the Black Forest was so common that many referred to it as "Sherwood Forest" in jest, and its reputation as an outlaw refuge became legendary.

With such a mysterious history of the ancient forest, it would be difficult to determine who haunts the Lee residence on Shoup Road. The property is considered the Holy Grail for ghost hunters, and professionals in the industry believe it to be the most haunted location in the United States.

When Steve and Beth Lee bought a cabin in the Black Forrest back in 1991, they had no idea that the land was haunted—by what, no one can say exactly. The Lees have stressed that they do not believe in ghosts and were baffled when their home was plagued by strange chemical odors just a month after moving in. When poltergeist activity in the home became violent, Mr. Lee spent thousands of dollars on a security system. The family was flabbergasted when phantom images of dogs, human faces and ghostly fatigue-clad soldiers appeared on the monitors. Mr. Lee was convinced that the government had something to do with it, though he swears he doesn't believe in conspiracy theories. Many people thought the Lee family was collectively crazy until a show called *Sightings* televised three separate investigations at their home. The producers concluded that something unexplainable was going on in their neck of the woods and determined it had to be paranormal in nature. A Hopi Indian shaman informed the Lee family that the sacred forest had a rainbow vortex surrounding it and explained that there are only two other rainbow vortexes on the entire planet. The medicine man was sent to do a spiritual cleansing of the home and discovered that the cabin was built over a portal between the physical and spiritual worlds as well.

According to the *Rocky Mountain News*, Colorado state senator Charles Duke visited the Lee residence because he didn't believe the ghost stories. The skeptical senator even took his own camera and another witness with him to do a thorough investigation of the mysterious property. After viewing pictures he took of orbs and beams of light, the senator concluded that something "bizarre" was going on at the little cabin in the woods.

If you have always wanted to own a haunted house, barn and spooky acreage of your very own, the Lees' ghostly digs are now on the market. Real estate brokers have the home listed with a firm price and an appropriate *caveat emptor*: buyer beware. This property is very haunted.

More information about the strange haunting can be found online by searching for Black Forest/Lee residence. Fascinating recorded evidence of the most haunted house in America can also be seen on the YouTube website.

For more information on the Palmer Divide area, visit the Palmer Lake Historical Society and Museum at 66 Lower Glenway in Palmer Lake or visit its website at PalmerDivideHistory.org.

Spirits of Pikes Peak and Garden of the Gods

All our times have come
Here but now they're gone
Seasons don't fear the reaper
Nor do the wind, the sun or the rain.
—Blue Oyster Cult, "(Don't Fear) The Reaper"

Colorado College professor Catherine Lee Bates penned the poetic song "America the Beautiful" while gazing at the prairie from the precipice of Pikes Peak. The popular patriotic anthem provoked many to start calling the majestic peak "America's Mountain," and the moniker has stuck ever since. Over the years, much has been written about the beloved mountain, including mysteries, legends, tall tales and, of course, ghost stories.

Some of the tall tales about Pikes Peak began in 1873, when army sergeant Robert Seybroth was stationed to live alone at the weather station built on top of the peak. One may never know why the soldier began fabricating the fantastic tales; perhaps it was loneliness, boredom or the high altitude. Regardless of the reason, he gained a lot of attention when his outlandish reports made international headlines. One afternoon, Seybroth reported that while peering through his telescope he spied a gigantic sea monster swimming below in the cold waters of Mystic Lake (now called Lake Moraine). He claimed that the green-scaled serpent was nearly one hundred feet long and devoured land animals by snatching them from the shoreline with the flick of its tongue. News of the gigantic slurping serpent alarmed

8464. Station on Summit of Pike's Peak, Colo.

An antique postcard depicting the weather station on the summit of Pikes Peak. *Author's collection.*

locals and tourists wanting to climb the mountain because they feared being eaten by the raging reptile.

Another Irishman named Sergeant John Timothy O'Keeffe replaced Seybroth in 1875 and was soon telling whoppers that remarkably trumped his predecessor. The *Rocky Mountain News* reported in 1876 that Sergeant O'Keeffe's family was attacked by legions of vicious man-eating mountain rats while living on the summit. Thankfully, they were able to stave off the vile creatures with chunks of raw meat until they managed to rig a wire and electrocute the rowdy rodents. Their baby daughter, Erin O'Keeffe, however, was tragically devoured by the voracious varmints before her parents could come to her rescue. A sad photo of the baby's funeral on the rocky summit was posted in newspapers across the nation, and mailbags stuffed with sympathy cards addressed to the grieving parents soon followed. Later, it was learned that O'Keeffe wasn't even married, and the prankster was reprimanded for the preposterous joke. However, the scorned soldier kept his position on the mount until four years later, when his apparent need for attention propelled him to report that a volcano had suddenly erupted on the summit of Pikes Peak. He claimed that he was nearly killed when he got within two hundred feet of the explosion, which doused him with thick ash, and added that the frightening experience reminded him of a time that he was sprayed with soot when Mount Vesuvius erupted in his native land of Italy. O'Keeffe fooled everyone once again with his outlandish tale, and no one even questioned the redheaded, freckle-faced soldier about his Italian heritage.

Ghost stories about Pikes Peak were first told by the Native Americans, who believed that the mysterious lights seen on the mount were supernatural beings known as lightning spirits. These strange mystical orbs were also seen by the earliest explorers in the region. According to the *Gazette Telegraph*, the luminous lights looked like glowing balls of fire being tossed around the mountain and were visible as far east as the prairie town of Falcon. The earliest pioneers also witnessed the strange wonder and called it St. Elmo's fire. Regional miners said the strange phenomenon looked like ghost lights and believed that it was the souls of fellow comrades killed on the mountain while hunting for gold.

One of these miners was J.G. Hiestand, an entrepreneur who worked at the summit house on Pikes Peak. The affable businessman was well known for spinning yarns and told tourists that the ghost lights came from the lantern of an old friend who had died on the mountain. Hiestand claimed that the miner fell into a bottomless pit on the south side of the summit and was thought to be lost forever until his ghost appeared on the mountain. The old man's skeleton held a glowing lantern and wandered the mountain, warning all about the perilous dangers lurking there. Years later, old Hiestand himself was said to haunt the peak after he died under suspicious circumstances. His skeletal specter is still seen walking side by side with his old mining pal, and he, too, carries a guiding lantern. Another spooky story about the peak tells about a naked hitchhiking ghost who is often seen near mile marker thirteen. "Desperation Mona" is usually seen just before dusk standing by the road, soaking wet, with her thumb stuck out begging for a ride. However, when motorists stop to pick her up, she usually disappears; however, she has been known to accept a ride now and then, much to the alarm of unwitting tourists!

The scariest ghost story about the infamous mountain would be hard to believe if it weren't actually proven to be true. The drama began in Dallas, Texas, which locals claim is so hot in the summer that you can fry an egg on a sidewalk. Perhaps the heat is what sent Mr. William A. Skinner and his wife, Mrs. Skinner, running for the hills. Mrs. Skinner, an athletic woman, was determined to climb Pikes Peak while on vacation. Mr. Skinner was a good ten years older than his forty-five-year-old wife and was not as keen about challenging himself as she was. However, he gave in to her desperate wishes and probably figured that physically exerting himself for a few hours was far more favorable than listening to her gripe about her disappointing Colorado vacation for the rest of his life.

On the morning of August 22, 1911, the duo had breakfast, shopped and did some sightseeing in Manitou Springs. It wasn't until noon that they began their ascent up Pikes Peak on that beautiful late summer day. Witnesses later recalled noticing the Skinners trekking up Ruxton Avenue toward the cog railroad depot in light summer clothing. A shopkeeper assumed that the stylish-looking, color coordinated twosome was going on an afternoon picnic but noted that they didn't carry provisions with them. At about four o'clock in the afternoon, a cog train going down the mountain passed the Skinners. One of the passengers later recalled a tall, skinny woman and her short, pudgy, lagging companion and remembered how comical it was when she yelled back at him with a strong southern twang, "I came here all the way from Dallas, Texas, and I said we were going to climb Pikes Peak, and that is exactly what we are going to do!"

An hour later, the sky darkened, and the wind began to howl, but the duo pushed forward and managed to make it to the halfway house by late afternoon. There, the couple rested in the rustic lodge for a few minutes among fellow travelers, all better equipped and headed in the opposite direction. Mr. Skinner begged water from a stranger and almost burst into tears when he saw the man throw a half-eaten sandwich to the birds. When he began complaining about discomfort, his demanding wife admonished him for being a killjoy. One hiker heading downhill warned them about the changing weather, but the determined Texans agreed to soldier on anyway. As they left the safety of the mountain cabin, Mr. Skinner is remembered to have said, "OK, Dearie, we will keep going until we get to the top. I will die game if I have to."

The next morning, the Texans were discovered not far from the cog tracks near Windy Point, hiding under a large boulder and a foot of snow. Tragically, the frozen fanatics were less than a half mile from the summit when they had succumbed to hypothermia in a blinding blizzard the night before. Mr. Skinner was found lying down with his head propped up on a rock pillow; his arms were folded across his chest, and he appeared to be sleeping. His wife, however, portrayed a more tragic figure, sitting upright with her eyes frozen into a blank stare and a single teardrop frozen to her chalk-white cheek. The tortured woman must have been haunted with regret as she waited for Jack Frost and the Grim Reaper to end her horrific suffering. Authorities were alerted, and a special cog train was sent to retrieve the frozen stiffs. Among the couple's few possessions were a couple postcards and some small change. Unbelievable as it sounds, inside Mr. Skinner's jacket pocket was a letter dated August 17, 1911, from Mr. J.H. Choice that read, "I hope that you are having the time of your life in Colorado. I am sending you an overcoat as per your request. I hope you don't freeze to death on Pikes Peak."

Ironically, the other envelope in his possession was a life insurance policy, which was ruled invalid if death was caused by overexertion.

The press had a field day with the strange story of the Skinners' untimely deaths. Sadly, few newspapers were sympathetic about their demise, and most were downright mean. One Texan newspaper, the *Cleburne Morning Review*, commented on August 23 about the unseasonable hot weather and joked that it might be pleasant to freeze to death in the mountains like the Skinners rather than suffer through being "stewed, fried or boiled" in the southern heat wave.

Local authorities speculated that Mrs. Skinner could have probably saved herself but remained loyal to her husband with the fierce pride of a lioness until the bitter end. However, they agreed that her arrogance is what got her into the deadly situation in the first place and noted that pride always comes before a tragic fall. There is an old mountaineer legend that says that people who perish in the wilderness from pride die in shame. Perhaps that is why the proud Texans still haunt the area near Windy Point to this day. Several hikers over the years have claimed to see the frightening apparition of the frozen fanatics huddling under the large boulder near Windy Point. Over one hundred years later, the spooky cautionary tale about the foolhardy Texans is still told to warn others not to mess around with Mother Nature. The Manitou Springs Heritage Center hosted a tour up Pikes Peak on the cog train to commemorate the 100th anniversary of the Skinners' fateful climb. It is not known if anyone saw the ghosts of the Skinners under the rock shelter at Windy Point that day, but it can be certain that everyone on board brought a warm coat.

Paranormal investigators agree that the coup de grâce of haunted tourist destinations is the Garden of the Gods. American Indians revere the park as sacred and have been making pilgrimages to the ancient burial ground for centuries. Well known for its towering sandstone formations and breathtaking vistas, the glorious property was purchased by Charles Perkins and gifted to the City of Colorado Springs on Christmas Day 1909; Perkins graciously stipulated that it always be free and open to the public. Sunrise has long been a popular time for photographers. When

Ute Indian Camp, Garden of the Gods, Colo.

An antique postcard of the gateway rocks in the Garden of the Gods. *Author's collection.*

the light of dawn strikes the three-hundred-foot-tall red rocks, the colors are absolutely gorgeous against the bright blue sky. Perhaps the natural beauty of the park is why General William Palmer cherished riding his horses there. Palmer lived just a mile away at the lovely castle he built for his family called Glen Eyre. In 1906, Palmer fell from his horse near the gateway rock in the Garden of the Gods and was mortally injured. Tragically, he suffered from debilitating paralysis and died three years later. Does the founding father of Colorado Springs haunt the famous red stone park? No one really knows for certain, but professional psychics believe that the park is haunted by legions of spirits, some nearly as old as the rocks themselves.

Despite vast archaeological research, the ancient holy ground is still shrouded in mystery. In the late 1800s, a mysterious cavern known by early pioneers as "Echo Cave" was discovered inside the gateway rock that was believed to have sheltered the Lawrence party during a thunderstorm in 1858. The early pioneers left graffiti inside the cavern alongside ancient Indian hieroglyphics. In 2008, historian and activist Dave Hughes tried to get a grant to have the cave excavated and documented. However, American Indian leaders refused to give researchers permission to invade the holy shrine of their ancestors; thus, the mouth of the cave was sealed to keep its secrets safe for all eternity.

Gazing at the formidable sky-scraping rock formations with names like the Three Graces, Twin Sisters and Balanced Rock is quite inspirational. However, climbing the rocks (without a permit) is not only dangerous but also illegal. Dozens of unfortunate awestruck visitors, lured by the towering passion of the Kissing Camels, have accidently plunged to their deaths. Despite the posted warnings, Spiderman wannabes look at the perilous rocks as eye candy and often ignore the signs. Tragically, it seems like every summer an unwitting victim is sacrificed to the blood-red cliffs of the gods, and paranormal enthusiasts lament that some tourists leave more than just their hearts behind in the beloved park.

Ghost busters in the know will tell you that the Garden of the Gods Trading Post is the mother lode of haunted hot spots. The historical landmark was once the longest-operating trading post in the country. The enterprise began in the early 1900s, when an industrious ten-year-old kid named Charles E. Strausenback began carving and selling gypsum figures to tourists at the east entrance of the park near Fatty Rice's Beer Hall. By 1924, the young entrepreneur had saved enough money to build the trading post at the southwestern entrance of the park. He studied southwestern architecture and then devised the structure to resemble a pueblo home, complete with adobe fireplace and wrought-iron fixtures. The bilingual German also learned several Indian dialects so that he could competitively trade with local tribes. Two large hogans were built nearby for the Navajo Indian families who farmed the land. Strausenback hired American Indian dancers to entertain tourists and craftsmen from local tribes to sell their wares at the curio museum. Handmade Pueblo Indian pottery and baskets were very popular with tourists, as were Navajo blankets and sterling silver Indian jewelry. Strausenback had the Midas touch and turned the inspired endeavor into a booming business. However, not long after tasting the sweetness of success, old Charlie was run out of town on federal bootlegging charges. After his death, the Garden of the Gods Trading Post was rumored to be haunted. Could the entrepreneur be haunting his former labor of love?

Operating manager Laszlo Palos heard whispers about the "phantom customer" that regularly wreaked havoc on the old trading post at night and thought it was just a harmless joke. Employees reported that the art gallery, gift shop, picnic garden and snack bar would be in order upon leaving for the evening; however, the next morning, it looked like the post had a "Moonlight Madness" sale. Trinkets, postcards and books were scattered about, and employees were at a loss to explain the mystery. Mr. Palos affirmed that he still didn't believe in ghosts, despite the intriguing rumors. One night, when he was locking up, he saw the strange shadow of a human form walk from north to south about fifty feet in front of him. He said the apparition looked like a mirage, and it disrupted the air—a cold spot lingered where the image was seen, despite the summer heat. Curiosity compelled him to call in professionals, and Dorothy Tunnicliff, founder and lead investigator of Colorado Springs Ghost Hunters, answered the call. Along with co-founder Chris Cherry and investigators Vanessa McDonald, Don McDonald, Ben Welch, Alex Turner and Vickey Leiker, Tunnicliff conducted a private investigation.

Meters, cameras, recorders and a crew of trained professionals were stationed around the old trading post, and the team's dedication paid off in spades. A secret mystery about a former caretaker who committed suicide there over forty years ago was revealed with an incredible EVP recording. The Colorado Springs Ghost Hunters displayed their astonishing evidence at the annual October "Ghosts of the Post" Halloween event in the fall of 2011. If you don't like cliffhangers, check out the team's website at csghosthunters. com. (Just for the record, Mr. Palos still does not believe in ghosts but admits that the evidence was, in his words, "interesting.")

The park offers several free guided nature tours in the morning and afternoon. Other programs like the falcon watch and evening bat walk are also very popular. But if you really want a thrill, rent a Segway at the Garden of the Gods Visitors' Center on Thirtieth Street. The rental fee includes driving instructions and a helmet, making it a safe and fun way to tour the world's largest rock garden.

The Rockledge Ranch, located next to Garden of the Gods, is a historic homestead and living history museum that demonstrates life in the 1800s and has been placed on the National Register of Historic Places. This place is a real gem for history buffs and ghost hunters alike.

THE OTHERS

Hold on, man. We don't go anywhere with "ghost," "scary," "spooky," "creepy,"
"haunted" or "forbidden" in the title.
—Shaggy to Scooby Doo

THE CREEPY CITY AUDITORIUM

The Colorado Springs City Auditorium at 221 East Kiowa Street was added
to the National Register of Historic Places in 1996. The old grande dame
has seen many famous faces, including Dick Clark, Johnny Cash and the
Harlem Globe Trotters. Built in 1923, only a privileged few were in the
know about the secret subterranean tunnels that connected it to the police
station, city hall and the morgue. City officials used the tunnels of the
underworld to secretly venture to the auditorium after hours. There they
could openly drink moonshine and gamble with their cohorts. Legend tells
that the manager of the building was involved in a bootlegging ring, which
led him to be bludgeoned to death in the caretaker's apartment. His corpse
was taken to the basement and thrown into the gigantic boilers, along with
two other bodies that were incidentally still alive when they were sacrificed
to the hellish inferno. The remains of the three victims were never found,
and neither was proof that this story actually happened. I contacted a retired
Colorado Springs police detective who confirmed that he had heard the
rumor but had never run across proof that it actually happened. However,

he added that it does not mean that the murders didn't occur. It's quite possible that the embarrassing situation was "hushed" and swept under the rug by the so-called good old boys club.

Perhaps the building's haunted reputation had something to do with renaming the Little London Theater inside the City Auditorium after famous horror movie actor Lon Chaney. The favorite son of Colorado Springs was born in the city on April Fools' Day in 1883, which was befitting since he soon became a jokester. Chaney enjoyed making people on the streets laugh with his uproarious impersonations of local characters, like drunken Judge Baldwin. Chaney's parents were both deaf, which fostered his gift for pantomime from an early age, and he became world renowned as the "Man with a Thousand Faces." Lon Chaney was one of the most famous actors of his time and was perhaps best known for his role as the Phantom of the Opera. The Lon Chaney Theater is reportedly haunted by the celebrity, and some joke that it is he who plays the huge antique pipe organ housed under the stage. A few maintenance workers over the years have told about the old Wurlitzer organ playing haunting music at night when no one else is in the building. Could the spooky music be a ghostly performance by the city's very own phantom of the opera?

If anyone could answer that question, it would be the SpiritChasers paranormal investigation group headed by Christopher Allen Brewer and his partner, James Manda. The dynamic duo formed the paranormal investigation team after a strange experience in the City Auditorium that ended up hurling them into the national spotlight. All the hoopla began five years ago, when the accidental celebrities had the creative idea to make a DVD that would serve as a Halloween party invitation. Brewer and Manda were filming some footage in the City Auditorium when they accidently captured all kinds of ghost orbs, streaks of light and other paranormal activity. The evidence was so startling that they were flown to Los Angeles to film an episode for the Biography Channel's program *My Ghost Story*. The amateur ghost hunters had so much fun that they went pro, and the SpiritChasers set sail for the big horizon.

In April 2012, the team scored again when it appeared on *My Ghost Story* with evidence collected in Manitou Springs at the Cave of the Winds. The two ghost hunters joke about their launch into paranormal stardom and have continued to host the private Halloween party at the City Auditorium ever since they hit the big time. The highlight of the special event is a movie of all the paranormal evidence that the team has collected over the previous year. Christopher and James firmly believe that the City Auditorium is one of the most haunted spots in Colorado Springs and have collected volumes of evidence to prove it. For more information on their ghost hunts, you can view their blog, which details their paranormal adventures, at thespiritchasers. blogspot.com.

Want to hear the mighty Wurlitzer organ and possibly see a ghost? Summer Sack Lunch Serenades are presented by the Pikes Peak Area Theatre Organ Society. For more information, please call (719) 385-6581.

The Haunted Antlers Hotel

Queen Palmer named the first fine hotel in town the Antlers after the elk horn hat racks in the lobby. Built in 1883, the hostelry enjoyed only fifteen years of success before it was consumed in flames. Several people were killed in the raging blaze that was ignited from a cinder of a passing train. The hotel was rebuilt on an even grander scale in 1901, and the castle under Pikes Peak brought visitors from all over the world. The Antlers reigned over downtown Colorado Springs until it was razed in the 1960s in the name of progress. The new Antlers Hotel is built on the same spot, and some folks claim it is haunted by former guests, including two suicides and one murder victim. Others joke that the fine hotel is haunted by a former affable character known as Judge Baldwin, whose namesake bar is located near the lobby. Baldwin was a drunken farmer known for riding a donkey into town and for politicking from a soapbox. In 1868, he was attacked by Indians where the Antlers Hotel now stands, but the savages set him free when they discovered he had already been scalped once before. Ironically, he escaped the wrath of the murderous Indians only to die a few weeks later at the bottom of a water well. The joke went around town that the judge drowned by the very liquid he had refrained from drinking his entire life. But no one was laughing when it was discovered that the judge had possibly been murdered. Police found it suspect that the victim's pockets were turned inside out and his bank bag was missing. Not long after the judge's funeral, several folks saw the phantom of the drunken farmer stumbling around town, and the ghost stories about Judge Baldwin flourished. Some folks at the Antlers claim that the ghost of old Baldwin still bellies up to the bar now and then—a century after his fatal swan dive.

One of the Antlers' legacies is the ghost stories that were left behind after 129 years of business.

Gerry Murphy volunteers at the Old Colorado City Historical Society and conducts haunted tours of the downtown Colorado Springs area during the month of October. The Antlers Hotel is one of his favorite haunted hot spots. More information about his tours and historical presentations can be obtained at CallMurphy.com.

THE SPOOKY BROADMOOR

It's the world's tallest tombstone, but Spencer Penrose named it the "Will Rogers Shrine of the Sun" instead. Will Rogers was an American humorist, actor and politician from Oklahoma whose homespun charm and witticisms earned him legions of fans, one of them being the blue-blooded Philadelphian Spencer "Speck" Penrose. The unlikely friendship blossomed after just a short time, and when Rogers was killed in a tragic plane crash over Alaska, Speck named the monument in his honor. The singing tower chimes two thousand feet above the city of Colorado Springs, and its delightful song can be heard throughout the Broadmoor area. Remarkably, the 114-foot-tall shrine was built from a single slab of Cheyenne Mountain granite and was constructed without the use of any nails or wood. Speck and his wife,

An antique postcard of the Broadmoor Hotel. *Author's collection.*

116

Julie, are interred in the chapel of the shrine on the lower level. Mr. and Mrs. Penrose were instrumental in the development of Colorado Springs. In fact, the Cheyenne Mountain Zoo, located lower on the mountain, was built by Speck, as were the Pikes Peak Highway, the Broadmoor Hotel, Pauline Chapel and the El Pomar Foundation.

On October 31, 2004, the *Colorado Springs Gazette* listed the Will Rogers Shrine of the Sun in the top ten creepiest locations in town, noting that the colossal monument looks haunted with its spiraling towers reminiscent of Dracula's Castle.

THE SCARY GHOST TOWN WILD WEST MUSEUM

The Ghost Town Museum located on Highway 24 and Twenty-first Street will give you a unique peek into the past. Once you walk into the building, you are transformed into another dimension because, believe it or not, a replica of an old frontier town has been built inside the building, complete with a barbershop, apothecary, saloon and every other kind of business you might expect to find. (Except for brothels, because this place is rated PG.) Thankfully, the streets are lined with boardwalks so that the ladies don't have to drag their long skirts through the imaginary mud and horse dung. This place is more fun than a barrel of monkeys, but is it haunted? Some folks think so; in fact, several ghost-hunting clubs have rented the facility to hold investigations and have posted their evidence online.

It stands to reason that the fun-filled museum could be haunted because it was once part of the Midland Railroad yard. According to the Old Colorado History Center, there were a couple unsolved murders and several accidental deaths that happened in the old Midland yard. One worker fell head first into a vat of molten lead, and another was impaled when he jumped from the train and accidently landed butt first on a fence post (you know that had to hurt!). With all the tragic deaths, it's easy to say that the place could have a hotheaded or stuck-up ghoul lurking about.

THE FORBIDDEN CENTRAL UNITED METHODIST CHURCH

"A hole in the ground" is what congregants at Tourist Memorial Mission called their church on South Nevada Avenue for five years until it was completed. Memorial Mission only had money to dig the basement, and that's where they held their services until the rest of the church could be built in 1917. The building has had several incarnations since its holy days. The most diabolical owner was alleged gangster Joe Bonicelli, who owned the Pearl of Allah, the largest freshwater pearl, worth millions of dollars. The church is now the office of the *Colorado Springs Independent* newspaper and is reported to be very haunted. The most frequently seen specter is of a nice-looking young man who is spotted on the main level of the building reading a book. Witnesses have identified the ghost in an obituary photograph that was found in an old church scrapbook. He is believed to be Walter G. Schaefer, one of the first pastors of the church, who was fresh out of seminary school in 1916, when he took the pulpit. The Rocky Mountain Paranormal Research Society did an investigation of the building in 2006 and confirmed that it is haunted.

THE SCARY CITY HALL AND FIRE STATION

The Colorado Springs City Hall at 107 North Nevada Avenue is supposedly haunted by a ghost who got caught with his pants down—literally. The ghost is known as George, a former policeman who accidently shot himself in the crotch when he hung his gun holster on the back of the bathroom door. George has been hanging around since the 1940s and is known to play practical jokes. He likes to hide things from employees, especially their cellphones. Perhaps George doesn't like all the noise. However, he should be used to it by now because the basement of the building was once used as a shooting range. When the building was being remodeled in 2001, sounds of guns firing startled some of the construction crew working in the basement because they were unaware of the building's haunted history.

A fire warden known as "Old John" haunted the station near city hall. John lived to a ripe old age; however, his ghost started showing up at the fire station shortly after his death. One article in the *Gazette* published in 1909 wrote about how wiretapping on the fire alarm happened for months after Old John died, even though it was not even connected. The mystery deepened

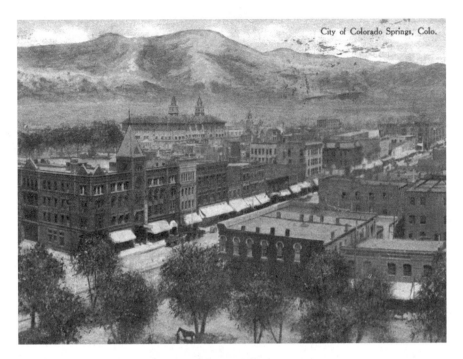

An antique postcard of downtown Colorado Springs. *Author's collection.*

when the tappings were deciphered as coming from fire box number thirty-three, which didn't even exist. However, several people remembered that thirty-three had been the warden's badge number. The article went on to say that the firemen were at a loss in understanding the strange mystery.

THE CREEPY GHOST GIRL AT LOWELL SCHOOL

Lowell School was built in 1892 and was the biggest school in Colorado Springs by 1910, with over one thousand students. The red brick Romanesque-style building at 831 South Nevada Avenue is now used as offices for the Colorado Springs Housing Authority and is home to a few ghosts, as well. One of them is believed to be a little girl named Nellie Ferguson, a former ten-year-old student who mysteriously disappeared from the school grounds back in September 1917 and was never seen or heard from again. It was called the biggest manhunt that the city had ever seen when hundreds of volunteers spent day and night searching for the redheaded, freckle-faced kid. Not long after she disappeared, several of her classmates claimed to have seen little Nellie playing on the schoolyard wearing her favorite pink dress. Still others attested to seeing their old friend skipping down the hallways. School administrators admonished these children for being insensitive and asked them to stop talking about the haunting on school property. However, when years went by and incoming students described the same apparition, staff took notice. It is believed that only other children can see the ghost of Nellie, and she is often seen playing on the playground and skipping down the hallways to this very day.

SKY-HIGH GHOST CASTLES

The Union Printers Home is a lovely red stone castle built on top of the hill overlooking downtown Colorado Springs back in 1892. The imposing structure sits on the corner of Union Boulevard and Pikes Peak Avenue and was built as a hospital and nursing home for members of the International Typographical Union. Mailers and printers worked in a risky profession, as many suffered and later died from the dreadful black lung disease. The illness was contracted by inhaling carcinogens, including coal dust and carbon-based ink. Essentially, victims were slowly poisoned over time, and it is safe to say that death by ink was not a pretty way to go. Madness often claimed patients long before sweet merciful death, and the wait for the Grim Reaper was agonizing. The lingering painful illness caused several victims to leap from the sky-scraping turrets to their deaths. The gruesome phantoms seen after the unfortunate suicides forever dog-eared the hospital as being haunted. When a murder happened there in 1907, the grisly reputation of the historic landmark was cemented for all eternity, especially after the ghost of Don Ferguson was seen wandering the hallways with a meat clever stuck in his head. The middle-aged man was clubbed by fellow wheel (bicycle) enthusiast, Jack Harris in the grand hallway. With friends like that, who needs enemies?

A neighboring historical landmark building is the Colorado School for the Deaf and Blind, which has been located on the corner of Kiowa and Institute Streets for nearly 140 years. The institution was built by Jonathan R. Kennedy out of necessity because three of his children were born deaf. His daughter Emma Kennedy married a deaf barber named Frank, and they became the proud parents of famed silent movie actor Lon Chaney. The Deaf and Blind School has been called a miniature Hogwarts; it looms over the Shook's Run neighborhood like a castle in the sky. Local lore tells that the building is haunted by a former teacher who died of tuberculosis at the turn of the century. Mr. Harris loved to get his hands dirty and often volunteered in the community garden. His ghostly figure has been seen many times walking around the expansive lawns and gardens that still surround the beautiful building.

THE FORBIDDEN LILLER MANSION

This once-glorious home near Bristol Elementary School could now be called the Mystery Mansion and looks like the kind of spooky place that Scooby Doo and Shaggy would be afraid to visit. The decaying mint green manor on Walnut Street hides behind several cardboard signs that are spray-painted in bright orange: NO TRESPASSING! The overgrown property is littered with broken-down cars, refrigerators and rusted bathtubs; hence, one gets the feeling that some toothless hillbilly is waylaid in the bushes just begging for an excuse to use his rifle. A weird sign posted on the barn and another by an old windmill scream: "TRESPASSERS WILL BE…HOT!!!" Upon closer examination, it appears that some troublemaker with a strange sense of humor painted over the missing "S" on both signs.

It is now hard to believe that this sad-looking house was once the epicenter of all social activity in the neighborhood and maybe even Colorado Springs to boot. Children, as well as barnyard critters, frolicked in the fragrant apple orchard, and a tree-canopied lane led to its welcoming front gate. J.E. Liller, an editor for the town's first newspaper, wanted the house to look inviting when he designed it with numerous windows and sitting porches back in 1871. However, Mr. Liller did not keep his dream house for long and sold it to John Finlay, who moved in with his young bride in 1883. Tragically, Mr. Finlay died in a train accident just a year later, and his grieving widow did not want to live in the big house alone. So she had a cozy cottage built in the woods behind the mansion, which she christened the "Finlay Orchard addition," and she lived there in seclusion until her dying day. In 1909, the country estate was purchased by J.J. Hagerman, president of the Colorado Midland Railroad and a Colorado College benefactor. His granddaughter, Elinor Hagerman Llewellyn, was a well-known rodeo queen who dazzled

The old Liller Mansion. *Courtesy of Sita Ahlen.*

fans in the Pikes Peak or Bust Rodeo parades by wearing her trademark hot pink cowgirl costume with its matching rhinestone-encrusted cowboy hat.

Queen Elinor gave up her crown to take over the property, and everything in the neighborhood was hunky-dory until 1956. That was the year the mayor took away the free watering privileges in that neighborhood when a nearby irrigation canal was redirected to the city cemetery. The once courtly cowgirl became hostile and retaliated by refusing to water the lovely grounds of the estate. Sadly, weeds grew sky high and slowly strangled the apple orchard until it finally withered and died behind the old stone wall. Rumors were that Elinor became a recluse in the cottage just like her predecessor, Mrs. Finlay. Elinor died in 1994, and the abandoned mansion and Finlay Orchard addition sitting on the five-acre parcel are still owned by her estate. Folks in the neighborhood began calling the estate the "Grudge Mansion" and for years have claimed to see lights glowing in the creepy old house at night, even though it has not been occupied for nearly half a century.

THE STRANGE CLIFF DWELLER MUSEUM

Are you old enough to remember the old Winnebago commercials from the 1970s? A family of adventurous, amateur archaeologists power up the side of a mountain in a large motor home to explore ancient Anasazi cliff dwellings. Well, those commercials were filmed at the Manitou Springs Cliff Dwellers Museum located off Highway 24 near Cave of the Winds. The Cliff Dweller Museum was established in 1904 after the ancient Indian dwellings were transported from a canyon in the southern part of the state and installed under a cliff in Manitou Springs in order to protect the structure from further decay. The museum is one of the oldest tourist attractions in the state and opened its doors in 1907.

According to Internet blogs, the Cliff Dweller Museum is haunted by the spirits of Anasazi Indians who lived there long ago. Mysterious apparitions have been seen in the pueblo, as well as in the huge gift shop. I interviewed employee Jan Kirk, and she definitely believes the place is haunted. She explained that one day she saw a cloud of pink smoke drift across the gift shop in front of the elevators and added that there was electricity in the air, like you can feel during a lightning storm. She said she knew that the apparition had to be paranormal in nature but was not alarmed at its presence because it felt peaceful.

Hannah Ahlen agrees that the museum is haunted because she had a similar experience when she visited with her Girl Scout troop, only she saw the mysterious smoke floating over the case displaying archaic human skulls. Good thing the old bones are housed behind glass; otherwise, visiting pooches might be tempted to trot off with bonafide souvenirs. This place is very dog friendly; hounds are allowed everywhere that humans are, and that made my posse Jesse James and Wyatt Earp feel like very lucky dogs indeed.

HAUNTED MANITOU SPRINGS

The village of Manitou Springs is located at the foot of Pikes Peak and has long been known as a hotbed of spiritual activity. The American Indians believed that the mineral springs were a gift from the gods and thus considered the valley to be holy ground. There were five warring tribes that frequented the springs; however, they wiped off their war paint and put down their weapons when the entered the sacred valley. In the early

1900s, thousands of people flocked to Colorado in search of a cure for tuberculosis because the climate was ideal. Many believed that the mineral waters were helpful as well, and the town became a popular destination for patients. Manitou Springs was known to be haunted almost as soon as it was established, and legends of ghosts roaming the hillsides and establishments in town have become legendary. During the last weekend in October, the town holds the annual Emma Crawford Coffin Races, one of the biggest Halloween parties anywhere.

More information about the spook-riddled hamlet can be found in my first book, Haunted Manitou Springs.

BIBLIOGRAPHY

Aldridge, Dorothy. *Historic Colorado City: The Town with a Future.* Colorado Springs, CO: Little London Press, 1996.

Armstrong, Helen. *The Walking Tour: A Guide to Historic Old Colorado City.* Manitou Springs, CO: Text Pros, 2000.

Conte, William R. *The Cheyenne Mountain Story.* Colorado Springs, CO: Century One Press, 1988.

Crouch, Lois. *Pikes Peak Legends. The History of Nordrach Ranch.* N.p.: Pikes Peak Posse of the Westerners, 2008.

Davant, Jeanne. *Wellsprings: A History of the Pikes Peak Region.* Colorado Springs, CO: Gazette Enterprises, 2001.

Dody, Marilou. *Haunted Places in the Shadow of Pikes Peak.* Colorado Springs, CO: self-published, 2010.

Ellis, Amanda M. *The Colorado Springs Story.* Colorado Springs, CO: House of San Juan, 1978.

Galbraith, Harry. Article. *Colorado Springs Gazette Telegraph,* June 28, 1942.

Haverkorn, Dwight. *The Colorado Springs Homicide Index*. Colorado Springs, CO, 1998.

Hughs, David R. *Historic Old Colorado City*. Colorado Springs: Old Colorado City Historical Society, 1978.

MacKay, Elaine. *Pioneer Migration to the West*. Fountain, CO: Fountain Valley Historical Society and Museum, n.d.

Mackell, Jan. *Brothels, Bordellos and Bad Girls: Prostitution in Colorado, 1860–1930*. Albuquerque: University of New Mexico Press, 2008.

Martin, Mary Joy. *Twilight Dwellers, Ghosts, Gases and Goblins of Colorado*. Boulder, CO: Pruett Publishing Company, 2003.

Ogden, Tom. *The Complete Idiot's Guide to Ghosts and Hauntings*. Indianapolis, IN: Alpha Books, 1999.

Olsen, Robert C. *Speck: The Life and Times of Spencer Penrose*. Lake City, CO: Western Reflections Publishing Company, n.d.

Readers' Digest. *American Folklore and Legend*. Pleasantville, NY: Readers' Digest Association, Inc., 1978.

Sprague, Marshall. *The Life and Good Times of Colorado Springs, in the Newport Rockies*. Athens: Swallow Press/Ohio University Press, 1961.

Waters, Stephanie. *Haunted Manitou Springs*. Charleston, SC: Haunted America, a Division of The History Press, 2011.

Wilcox, Rhoda. *The Man on the Iron Horse*. Manitou Springs, CO: Martin Associates, 1959.

Womack, Linda. *From the Grave: A Roadside Guide to Colorado's Pioneer Cemeteries*. Caldwell, ID: Caxton Press, 1958.

ABOUT THE AUTHOR

Stephanie Waters attended Palmer, Coronado, Pikes Peak Community College and the University of Colorado at Colorado Springs and has a degree in liberal arts. In the 1980s, she started her own business as a professional storyteller. She traveled the world in the 1990s and went on haunted history tours wherever they were offered. Inspiration (or perhaps insanity) struck in 2002, and the self-described history geek opened Blue Moon Haunted History Tours, as well as a haunted bed-and-breakfast in Manitou Springs. The hearse-driving mountain mama then began operating Colorado Ghost Tours LLC, which does special ghost-hunting events and tours around the state. Stephanie was thrilled to become an author when she wrote *Haunted Manitou Springs* in 2011 and had so much fun that she begged The History Press to let her write another one about Colorado Springs. And the rest, as they say, is history.

Visit us at
www.historypress.net